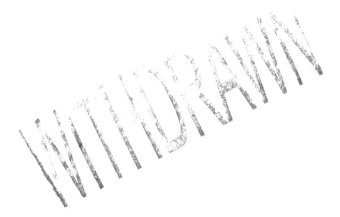

▶ Making the Moral Case for Social Sciences

DOI: 10.1057/9781137577917.0001

Also by Karl Spracklen

DIGITAL LEISURE, THE INTERNET AND POPULAR CULTURE (*2015*)

SOUNDS AND THE CITY (*co-edited with Brett Lashua and Stephen Wagg, 2014*)

WHITENESS AND LEISURE (*2013*)

CONSTRUCTING LEISURE (*2011*)

SPORT AND CHALLENGES TO RACISM (*co-edited with Jonathan Long, 2010*)

THE MEANING AND PURPOSE OF LEISURE (*2009*)

DOI: 10.1057/9781137577917.0001

palgrave▶pivot

Making the Moral Case for Social Sciences: Stemming the Tide

Karl Spracklen

Professor of Leisure Studies,
Leeds Beckett University, UK

palgrave
macmillan

DOI: 10.1057/9781137577917.0001

First published 2016 by
PALGRAVE MACMILLAN

Palgrave Macmillan in the UK is an imprint of Macmillan Publishers Limited, registered in England, company number 785998, of Houndmills, Basingstoke, Hampshire RG21 6XS.

Palgrave Macmillan in the US is a division of St Martin's Press LLC, 175 Fifth Avenue, New York, NY 10010.

Palgrave Macmillan is the global academic imprint of the above companies and has companies and representatives throughout the world.

Palgrave® and Macmillan® are registered trademarks in the United States, the United Kingdom, Europe and other countries.

ISBN: 978-1-137-57792-4 EPUB
ISBN: 978-1-137-57791-7 PDF
ISBN: 978-1-137-57790-0 Hardback

A catalogue record for this book is available from the British Library.

A catalog record for this book is available from the Library of Congress.

www.palgrave.com/pivot

DOI: 10.1057/9781137577917

Contents

Introduction

Abstract: *Spracklen sets out the problems social sciences have in comparison with the natural sciences in the modern world. The natural sciences (reduced to the acronym STEM) are seen as proper sciences by journalists and policy-makers because they find out true things about the world, make money and help governments solve problems. Spracklen establishes critical sociology as the theoretical framework through which he will analyse the relationship between the natural sciences and the social sciences, and through which he will make the moral case for social sciences in the rest of the book.*

Spracklen, Karl. *Making the Moral Case for Social Sciences: Stemming the Tide*. Basingstoke: Palgrave Macmillan, 2016. DOI: 10.1057/9781137577917.0002.

We are living in a neo-liberal age where the social sciences are under threat from a series of metaphorical tidal waves. First, there is the favouring of hard sciences or natural sciences (the STEM disciplines, named from the abbreviation for Science, Technology, Engineering and Medicine, currently used in academic policy circles – see Breiner, Harkness, Johnson and Koehler, 2012; Gough, 2014) in government policies and planning, whether in education and training, or the funding of research, because such forms of hard science are supposed to be of economic benefit to society (Fuller, 2000a). The use of the acronym STEM (a hard-sounding word, the main core of a plant holding the rest in place) has become common beyond academic policy circles, used by politicians and journalists to identify the important knowledge-makers. Second, there is a rise in interest among the public for popular science explanations of complex issues, which often translates into a crude scientism that reduces everything social and cultural to the biological. Third, there is a sustained, low-level attack on the social sciences and their legitimacy in higher education by populist politicians and writers. This right-wing critique of the social sciences is connected to the cultural wars of American civil society, but it has become transformed in our neo-liberal universities and funding councils into the rhetoric of impact and value, as described so forcefully by Thomas Docherty (2015) in his book *Universities at War*. In this system of Habermasian instrumentality (Habermas, 1984, 1987), all scholars are forced to demonstrate the worth of their research, and social sciences along with the humanities are naturally suspect in the eyes of university managers and government bureaucrats because of their supposed roots in the politics of the left (even though this is not the case), and their reluctance to find ways to make a profit out of critical thinking. The social sciences do not guarantee certain knowledge, do not offer solutions to problems that make money for corporations. The social sciences are compared to the sacred power of STEM, which brings the magic of profit as well as the certainty of truth and validity to intellectual inquiry, and are found wanting.

In response to these tides of 'STEM thinking', social scientists have tried to argue the value of their research and their disciplines. In the United Kingdom, for example, the Academy of Social Sciences has created a Campaign for Social Sciences, which includes themed reports that demonstrate to managers, policy-makers, politicians and journalists that social sciences can and do make an impact – that social sciences

DOI: 10.1057/9781137577917.0002

have value. But the nature of such arguments is undermined by the language of impact and value that the campaigners use. Fighting a battle to win the attention of sceptical policy-makers trained in neo-liberal ideology, the campaigners adopt the instrumental assumptions of hard science and capitalism. They say that the social sciences are as scientific as the hard sciences (i.e., their arguments are based on sound research and sound logic), and that the social sciences add value to the economy through the generation of patents, money-making ideas, businesses and skilled workers.

In this book I want to argue that this is a mistake. The social sciences should not use the language and concepts of neo-liberalism to make the case for the importance of social sciences. We have to stem this tide of instrumental logic, because it is taken from the systems of big science and global capitalism that have brought the struggle over diminishing resources in education and research to this crucial point. The social sciences cannot win this struggle by adopting the language of its rivals. The only way for the social sciences to survive is by making the moral case. I want to argue that the social sciences are necessary if humans are to live a freely communicative and moral life in a world dominated by hegemonic power, whether that power is built into belief systems, gender orders, popular culture, social classes or political constitutions. I want to argue that critical sociology, for so long the unfashionable discipline in social sciences, has a key role to play in resisting the instrumentality of other social sciences such as psychology and economics. In this book, I use the term 'critical sociology' to refer to that form of sociology that is inter-disciplinary and informed by the radical theories of scholars beyond sociology in cultural studies, political studies and philosophy. This critical sociology is not bound by its disciplinary name, but takes inspiration from the wider social sciences and humanities, and feeds into the social sciences. It is the critical social sciences exemplified by Marxism, radical feminism and Critical Race Theory, the kind of social scientific research and theorizing that identifies the truth about power inequalities in modernity. This critical thinking that accepts there is a truth to be found about the social world, and that truth is the fact of modern society's structures and constraints. So when I do talk about critical sociology, I am well aware that many of its best theorists and researchers are in related subject fields in the social sciences. And at the same time, I am aware that many sociologists reject this kind of critical, inter-disciplinary

DOI: 10.1057/9781137577917.0002

work for being too biased, or too political. Rather than follow the neo-liberal turn that has become normalized in the epistemologies of disciplines such as psychology and economics, critical sociology has always carried in it from Emile Durkheim through to C. Wright Mills, Jürgen Habermas and Stuart Hall about the importance of critical thinking. This ability to see the world through a critical lens is the necessary moral and social good that sociology gives to the social sciences, and through the social sciences to the wider world.

That is the purpose of this book. I want to show that the moral case for social sciences shows that they are not only important for the continued survival and development of global society, they are necessary. As such, this book should be of use to the following readers: campaigners defending social sciences in the public sphere; social scientists struggling to make their case for their courses in schools and universities; and students and academics who need to understand the weakness of the instrumental case and the strength of the moral case for social sciences, for their own writing. The short form of the Palgrave Pivot book series allows my argument to be to clear and to the point. In this book, the short form forces me to be concise and to handle carefully the inter-disciplinary theories that run through the argument I intend to make – the history and philosophy of science, sociology, politics and ethics – and also demands that the argument is in clear and simple language. This book is a unique contribution to the debate about the meaning and purpose of the social sciences, which is causing their practitioners to question their worth; and it will provide a strong moral justification for social sciences that rejects any attempt to put a price on them.

I am writing this book because I am a sociologist who works in an inter-disciplinary way across the humanities and social sciences to think about leisure and culture (Spracklen, 2009, 2011, 2013, 2015). But I am also by training a natural scientist with an interest and specialism in history and philosophy of science. This is clear from my published book *Constructing Leisure: Philosophical and Historical Debates* (Spracklen, 2011), which is a history and philosophy of leisure inspired by Habermasian ideas of communicative and instrumental rationality. Habermas argues that there are two major ways of thinking about the world: communicative rationality occurs when humans are free to discuss and inquire with one another about the world rationally; instrumental rationality is when the freedom of the inquiry is reduced to systems such as the 'bottom line' of economics, or the bureaucracies of corporations and nation-states. In my work on leisure, I have been interested in showing how leisure has been a communicative space, which has been subject to colonization by the commodification and commercialization that surrounds the modern leisure industry. This book uses the same framework and training to think about the struggle over the meaning and purpose of the social sciences. That is, I am interested in applying the split between communicative and instrumental rationality to exploring the rise of critical inquiry, the rise of natural science, the attack on social sciences and its instrumental defence, and the STEM thinking that dominates universities and education policy.

The first chapter, 'The Attack on Social Sciences', will chart the historical rise of the divide between the natural sciences and the social sciences, and the recent growth of big science and policies promoting STEM subjects. The chapter will be divided into three short sections and one final, longer section. The first section will explore the idea of 'science' (cautiously framed) from classical Greece, through medieval scholasticism, to the early modern period. The second section will explore the idea of 'science' in the Enlightenment and the construction of the public sphere, before charting the role of science (as we know it) in High Modernity. The third section will explore the divide of the sciences into the natural and the social in the past hundred and fifty years or so, and the subsequent de-valuing of the latter. The final section will describe the state of social sciences today, the dominance of STEM thinking and STEM policies and the attacks on the social sciences for not being 'proper' sciences that generate certain knowledge and economic growth. I will argue in this chapter that despite a certain suspicion about science in contemporary popular culture, and the denial of scientific knowledge on the fringes of far-right politics, the natural sciences retain a privileged place in the ways of thinking and ways of legitimizing knowledge and power in the modern world. STEM thinking makes as common-sense truth the contested claim that all human experience can be reduced to its economic value, and everything social can be reduced to the natural or discarded as false knowledge.

The second chapter, 'The Weakness of the Defence', will begin by setting out some of the more publicly argued responses or defences made by people about the legitimacy of the social sciences. I will then turn to arguments made historically about the instrumental value of the social sciences in the West, from the period of High Modernity in the late nineteenth century to the positivist turns in the second half of the twentieth

DOI: 10.1057/9781137577917.0002

century. I will show that the social sciences have been enthralled by two related ideas – the idea that the social might be measured by a slide-rule or computer; and the idea that the social sciences might be a tool to make governments work efficiently and industries make bigger profits. In the second half of the chapter the cases of economics, psychology and sociology will be explored and critiqued in more detail. I will show that economics is the moral exemplar of an over-confidence in scientific rhetoric and methods. I will show that the recent history of psychology is accommodation with natural sciences and the reductionist assumptions that the social can easily be explained as something natural, and something simple that can be monetized. I will show that sociology has faced similar pressures to follow the twin pressures of scientism and neo-liberalism. In the final section of the chapter I will show that the regimes of global capitalism, hegemony and governmentality that have taken over universities, education and government planning make the attempt to emulate STEM thinking in social sciences only serve to legitimize the instrumentality at the heart of this takeover. If social sciences make the case for their work and existence by measuring impact, measuring income generation and fetishizing scientific methods, they allow themselves to be the subject of reduction to the 'big' natural sciences, and allow themselves to be subsumed.

The third chapter, 'The Moral Case for the Social Sciences', will return to sociology to make the case that the ability to see the world through a critical lens is the necessary moral and social good that sociology gives to the social sciences, and through the social sciences to the wider world. The first section of the chapter will explore the history of the idea of critical thinking as a means to acquiring knowledge about the good life, from Greek philosophy through belief systems and into the radial, secular Enlightenment values of the public sphere. In the second section I will discuss sociological accounts of the importance of critical thinking, from Emile Durkheim, through C. Wright Mills, Michel Foucault and Stuart Hall to Jürgen Habermas. Then in the final section I will discuss the importance of critical thinking in the world in which we live, which is a world of enormous inequalities of power. I will argue that the social sciences are necessary and a moral and social good if humans are to live a freely communicative and moral life in a world dominated by hegemonic power, whether that power is built into belief systems, gender orders, popular culture, social classes or political constitutions.

DOI: 10.1057/9781137577917.0002

The concluding chapter will then look at the challenge we might have to ensure this notion of critical thinking and morality is not dismissed as utopian, idealistic or old-fashioned by the decision makers in education and the academy. I will suggest practical steps we might take to help social scientists resist the pressure to be instrumental in their work.

DOI: 10.1057/9781137577917.0002

1
The Attack on Social Sciences

Abstract: *Spracklen traces the divide between the natural sciences and the social sciences and the recent growth of big science. The chapter explores the idea of 'science' (cautiously framed) from classical Greece to today. The chapter shows the dominance of STEM thinking and the attacks on the social sciences for not being 'proper' sciences that generate certain knowledge and economic growth. Despite suspicion about science in contemporary popular culture, the natural sciences retain a privileged place in the ways of thinking and ways of legitimizing knowledge and power in the modern world. STEM thinking makes as common-sense truth the contested claim that all human experience can be reduced to its economic value, and everything social can be reduced to the natural or discarded as false knowledge.*

Spracklen, Karl. *Making the Moral Case for Social Sciences: Stemming the Tide.* Basingstoke: Palgrave Macmillan, 2016. DOI: 10.1057/9781137577917.0003.

DOI: 10.1057/9781137577917.0003

In this chapter, I chart the historical rise of the divide between the natural sciences and the social sciences, and the recent growth of big science and policies promoting STEM subjects. The chapter is divided into three short sections and one final, longer section. The first section explores the idea of 'science' (cautiously framed) from classical Greece, through medieval scholasticism to the early modern period. The second section explores the idea of science in the Enlightenment and the construction of the public sphere, before charting the role of science (as we know it) in High Modernity. The third section will explore the divide of the sciences into the natural and the social in the past hundred and fifty years or so, and the subsequent de-valuing of the latter. The final section will describe the state of social sciences today, the dominance of STEM thinking and STEM policies and the attacks on the social sciences for not being 'proper' sciences that generate certain knowledge and economic growth. I will argue in this chapter that despite a certain suspicion about science in contemporary popular culture, and the denial of scientific knowledge on the fringes of far-right politics, the natural sciences retain a privileged place in the ways of thinking and ways of legitimizing knowledge and power in the modern world. STEM thinking makes as common-sense truth the contested claim that all human experience can be reduced to its economic value, and everything social can be reduced to the natural or discarded as false knowledge.

The idea of science: it all begins with the Greeks

All cultures and societies think about their place in the world and the stuff that makes up the world. With our ability to think critically and abstractly, humans have tried to make sense of themselves and their surroundings as soon as were able to speak and draw (Gamble, 2007; Renfrew, 2008). Humans seem to have an innate desire to find causal relationships and regularities in the world, because much of pre-modern life depended on it: for example, where to find food and water at a particular time of the year; being able to know the time of the year; or knowing what berries were safe to eat. In other words, we have always developed two things: an ontology or metaphysics of the stuff around us; and an epistemology that gives us the tools to know the things we need to know about that stuff. The basic epistemological trick of assuming everything has a cause helps us realize that rain water causes our

DOI: 10.1057/9781137577917.0003

local wells to fill, but simple assumptions about causality lead us to think other things might be at work in our metaphysics. That is, we often make causal agents that do not exist in the desire to know why things happen (Harari, 2015; Wiseman and Watt, 2004). The rise of beliefs in magic and gods is associated with that impulse to know. This belief in magic is still with us today whenever anyone picks their lucky numbers for the lottery, or sits in the same seat on the bus every time they get on it. Such beliefs may not trouble many of us. For others, they are a distraction from our attempt to construct and epistemology that allows us to find out what is really happening in the world around us. This epistemology is science, loosely defined. That is, science in this section is taken to mean the search for truths about the world and everything in it that relies only on natural causes.

Popular histories about the rise of science and scientific thinking nearly always begin with the Greeks of the Classical Age such as Socrates, Plato and Aristotle – or bring them onto the page at a critical moment when humans reject falsehoods and faith for reason (there are too many to cover comprehensively, but for recent best-selling science histories see Bynum, 2013; Weinberg, 2015). This is because the Greek philosophers were strongly influential on the rise of the Western epistemological tradition, and Western science is based on Western epistemology (Russell, 2013). And Western science is the default science of the modern, global world, even as we enter an age of post-colonialism. It was the Greeks who wrote things down that have stayed with us, translated into Latin and/or Arabic, then back to Latin and then into modern languages. This knowledge has always been used to denote elite belonging, from their own age through the hegemony of the Roman Empire, and down to the West today, where Ancient Greek and Latin language, culture and thinking remain central to what it means to be an elite Westerner (ibid.). Of course, there are other inspirational systems of thinking that have survived through the transmission of those texts, such as those associated with Islam, Hinduism and the differing Chinese schools (Goonatilake, 1998). All of these have had varying degrees of impact on the Western epistemological tradition, but the truth remains that those impacts have been a result of appropriations and instrumental necessity, rather than inter-cultural dialogue.

It is also true to say then that the dominant ideology of science, loosely defined, begins with the Greek philosophers (Braund, 1994; Fox, 2005; Lane, 2015; Rhodes, 2003; Russell, 2013). Collectively, they wanted to account for and make sense of everything, from the motions of the planets and the precession of the spheres, through the limits of the divine, the causes of life and growth, the inner workings of animal and human bodies, and the right ways in which societies should be formed. For some of them (Socrates and Plato), what we see in the world is an illusion, a reflection of a purer Form or Divine Creator, which might be accessible through intense study of geometry and mathematics. For others (Aristotle), our everyday sense can be trusted to show us how the world is, and we can build up our knowledge of it through observation and collation of facts and stories. Importantly for the story about the rise of science, the Greeks developed and used a system of logical thought, which helped them to create rules about what they considered to be a good scientific argument.

In the Socratic dialogues, Plato shows us how clever Socrates is in his debating style with those who question him. Inevitably, interlocutors such as Glaucon fail to find flaws in Socrates's arguments, and they give ground to him. Socrates is our model and our method (Lane, 2015). He rejects rhetoric and fancy style. He shows us the steps he makes in his arguments, and the logical veracity that takes us from his premises to his conclusions. In Aristotle's hands, the Socratic method is combined with empiricism (Salkever, 2014). And like many of his forebears, Aristotle is also interested in applying philosophy to a wide range of subjects. This means he thinks science, loosely defined, should be able to explain everything within the ambit of our reason. So he writes books that look to us like modern, natural science, on things we might call astronomy or biology, for example. But he also writes books on things we might now reject as being part of science: political ethics and literary criticism, for example. The Greeks, then, invent this thing loosely defined as science, but their science is philosophy, and philosophy encompasses everything we do in our universities now, not just natural sciences, but social sciences and humanities. For the Greeks, they are all subjects of interest for the one epistemological tradition.

The Greeks are important to us because the study of philosophy becomes a compulsory part of the education of an elite Greek in the period, and when the Romans adopted Greek practices (just before they conquered them completely) they adopted their liberal education. Philosophy then becomes part of the Roman Empire's epistemological tradition, even if the more abstract philosophical problems are seen as less important to everyday elite Roman life than the art of rhetoric and

DOI: 10.1057/9781137577917.0003

practical engineering skills (Fox, 2005). All elite Roman men cultivate some knowledge of philosophy, and tell their children (mainly boys but sometimes girls) to be instructed in it. Some philosophical works are translated into Latin, others are copied in their original Greek and re-used. Not all Romans aspire to be known as great philosophers, such as the emperors Marcus Aurelius or Julian, but all elite men recognize philosophy's centrality to their system of learning (Morford, 2002). So the people who resurrect the liberal arts as part of their neo-classical, elitist education in the West in early modernity also resurrect the idea that philosophy, science loosely defined, is part of their epistemological toolkit (Fox, 2005; Russell, 2013).

But the Greek epistemological tradition survives not just because of the Renaissance and the rise of Western imperialism (and its effect on education and learning). It survives down to us because it is inherited, in highly contested and contextualized cases, in both Christianity and Islam. When Christianity grows to become the biggest and the official religion of the Roman Empire, its theologians adopt the critical skills of the classical liberal arts to their exegeses of the sacred texts. There are powerful voices that warn Christians to be wary of the scepticism and reason of the pagans, when faith alone should be above enough for a believer (McDonald, 1998). But Christian theology is suffused with philosophy from the neo-Platonism of Augustine down to the Aristotelian scholasticism of Thomas Aquinas. To understand theological arguments in early medieval Christianity, and to make them, one needs a thorough grounding in the Greek epistemological tradition. It is logic and metaphysics that allows the Christian to make sense of the created world and one's place in it. This need for a philosophical education disappeared in parts of the West, but continued in a simplified form through what we think of as the Dark Ages in enough cathedral schools and monasteries to sustain a Christian elite literate in Latin. Later, scholars started to attract pupils willing to pay attention to them talk, and to learn from them, which led to the formation of the medieval universities in Europe. The Western epistemological tradition that emerges in its mature form in the work of Aquinas cannot be anything other than scientific, because it is based on the laws of argument taken from the science of the Greeks, that is, from philosophy (Russell, 2013). Despite the concerns raised by other theologians and Christians in the period, scholasticism shaped the way modern science, in its loose definition, is now understood. It constructed the idea of the dissertation and disputation, the idea of the

DOI: 10.1057/9781137577917.0003

lecture and the idea that students learn in universities from scholars on degree courses (Hannam, 2010).

Muslims came into contact with Greek philosophy and Romano-Greek teachers of philosophy when they conquered large parts of the eastern Roman Empire in the seventh century. In the inter-cultural dialogue that took place, many Romano-Greeks traditions were adopted by the Arab rulers, especially as conversions started to take place among the Greek population still living in cities such as Damascus and Alexandria (Gutas, 2012). Many books of Greek philosophy were translated into Arabic, and a school of Islamic philosophy emerged that used the Greek science to make sense of Islam and the rest of the world (ibid.). Used to justify Islam, Greek philosophy was tolerated, but it was then used to question the claims made in Islam, and ultimately the root of critical inquiry was not tolerated (Leaman, 2013). But the Greek epistemological tradition survived enough in Arabic texts so that when scholasticism was at its height in Europe, Western scholars started to search for Greek authors preserved in purer forms in Arabic than the Latin ones that had survived the fall of the western Roman Empire (Grant, 1996; Russell, 2013). This was helped by Christian expansionism in Spain, when Muslim libraries and their contents fell to the conquerors. So the Western epistemological tradition survived and prospered because of Christianity and Islam.

The so-called scientific revolution

The idea of the 'scientific revolution' is one that can be read almost as soon as the Royal Society starts to publish its proceedings in the seventeenth century (Shapin, 1996). Although they do not talk about science, those scholars who call themselves natural philosophers see that the way they do natural philosophy has changed beyond recognition from the medieval scholasticism that preceded it (Hall and Dunstan, 1954). The valorization of Isaac Newton begins in his own lifetime, and his revolutionary contribution to the Western epistemological tradition becomes a dominant fact of history soon after his death (Westfall, 1983). By the nineteenth century, when William Whewell coins the term science for the subject of critical, natural philosophy, the idea that science and its methods emerged fully formed in early modernity, from the darkness of the previous ages, is taken as so obvious as to be unquestioned (Lightman, 1997; Yeo, 1993). Popular histories of science say this, as do histories of science written by scientists, as do scholars as far apart as Hegel and Nietzsche (Russell, 2013). Even in the history of science or the sociology of knowledge in the twentieth century, the scientific revolution is a given fact (Kuhn, 1962; Shapin, 1996).

The story basically says that there was a revolution in thinking about how we come to knowledge about the world in the seventeenth and early eighteenth centuries. Instead of assuming the authority of the classical philosophers or theologians, philosophers had to find things out for themselves. That is, they needed to make observations about the things they saw. At the same time, they needed to develop theories to explain the world, often based on mathematics, from which one could construct general laws about things (Kuhn, 1962; Westfall, 1977). For some natural philosophers it was enough to theorize from observational evidence and logical principles. But others argued that natural philosophy had to be based on experiments, interventions into the world that could be controlled by the philosopher. Technological developments and the rise of capitalism created material and financial resources for solving problems. This was the age of Galileo using the telescope to discover the moons of Jupiter, or Newton bending light with prisms (Westfall, 1983). This was also the age of reformation, which has been identified by Weber and Lindberg as a key factor in the rise of scientific thinking (Lindberg, 2009; Weber, 2001). Protestantism rejected authority and privatized the search for God precisely at the same time as humanists were finding new classical texts, and philosophers were searching for knowledge about the world around us without being grounded in Aristotelianism (Russell, 2013).

The scientific revolution, then, was said to have constructed modern science as it is known, both its practice, its method and its ethics. The science of this story is public, collaborative and experimental. It creates and tests hypotheses using a range of mathematical models and experimental procedures. Scientists publish their work and share their knowledge openly. Other scientists attempt to replicate the logic and the procedures to test if the findings and conclusions are correct. Scientific knowledge is cumulative, its ontology real and certain, because its epistemology is objective: science does tell us how things work.

There is no doubt that natural philosophy from the seventeenth century onwards constructs an impressive and useful body of knowledge. Universal laws such as that discovered by Boyle for the relationship between pressure and temperature of a contained gas prove themselves

DOI: 10.1057/9781137577917.0003

to be eminently useful for the burgeoning capitalist industries of the West. The appliance of such laws to the market-place allow individual engineers such as James Watt to transform society, and become incredibly wealthy (Dickinson, 2010). The rise of the West and the rise of the British Empire is strongly linked to the rise of modern science and its engineering applications (Lightman, 1997). Furthermore, the practice and ethics of natural philosophy contribute directly to the Enlightenment. Philosophers see their age as the modern age, the culmination of the rejection of medieval scholasticism and superstition and the embrace of reason. For the Enlightenment philosophers, Newtonianism provides proof for their attempts to transform society: feudalism, religion and vested interests have no place in the public sphere. As Habermas (1989) shows, the public sphere operates like the rooms of the Royal Society, or the coffee shops that were springing up in every major European city: men and women come together as equals in a communal enterprise to communicate and figure out problems.

In the last years of the twentieth century, historians of science started to unpick the traditional, epistemologically progressive but culturally elitist story of the scientific revolution. For some, the revolution happened over a longer period of time (Hall, 2014); for others the very idea of a revolution is misguided (Shapin, 1996). The changes in the Western epistemological tradition certainly happened. By the nineteenth century everybody knows what science is. But the passage from there to here is not as smooth as the story suggests. Newton, for instance, was not trying to remove God at all from philosophy; rather he was a committed believer who wrote extensively on biblical prophecies, and who also spent a large part of his life distracted by the irrational allures of alchemy (Mandelbrote, 1993). As far as this book is concerned, the other interesting thing about the philosophers associated with both the Scientific Revolution and the Enlightenment is their interest in the whole range of what the Greeks thought of as philosophy, or science, loosely defined. It is only a product of our divisions into our disciplines that we place Locke here, Hume and Kant there and Newton somewhere else. They all believed that they were engaged in the same sort of epistemological tradition, the one I have been calling the Western epistemological tradition, or science, loosely defined. Newton may have been obsessed with a few things such as optics and gravity that form the basis of modern physics, but many of the other big names of the period were involved in thinking about society and culture, the social sciences, as well as ethics,

DOI: 10.1057/9781137577917.0003

and how the heavens turn – as I discuss in more detail later on in this book. In the Enlightenment, this was even more obvious than in the seventeenth century. This was a time when Joseph Priestley and Erasmus Darwin might plan radical political reform, while in France other radical philosophers discussed and wrote manifestos demanding liberty, equality and fraternity (Habermas, 1989). Kant applies his methods to thinking about the social, the ethical, the political and the natural. The subject of Enlightenment philosophy was, then, considerably wider than the science of Whewell, or the science of today.

The rise of natural science and social science

Natural science started to be seen as economically vital in the period of high modernity, the nineteenth century onwards, when physics and chemistry, in particular, were providing laws and processes and materials that shaped modern society's switch to urbanization and the factory-production system. In Germany, the modern university system grew from the political recognition that industries needed recruits skilled in physics and chemistry (Scott, 2006). All over the West, scientific journals started to proliferate in number in the same period alongside scientific societies and associations. Universities on the German model, with PhD students and professors and their laboratories, emerged in major cities. Every Western power wanted its own scientists and engineers to find things out that would help the powers gain more power over their rivals. The technology and science of the West helped the expansion of empires and constructed both British hegemony, and American hegemony, on the ideology of free trade (Hobsbawm, 1988, 1989, 1992).

After Darwin's famous book *The Origin of Species* (1859, reprinted 2009), biology became as equally fashionable as physics and chemistry. In publishing *Origin* as 'one long argument', drawing on models and analogies to reach what Whewell called inductive consilience (Ruse, 1979; Yeo, 1993), Darwin was engaging in a debate within the imagined community of the British inheritors of the Newtonian programme (the imagined inheritance of an imagined Newton – the Newton as lone scientist elucidating the Divine) about the meaning of that programme. Whewell had used his position and influence in the Tory circles of Anglican science to define a good scientific law (a symbolic boundary) as a law that reconciled a number of problems (Yeo, 1993). But both Whewell and Herschel had set out limits to what the Newtonian programme could be applied (Depew and Weber, 1995). The boundary was defined through natural theology, following Paley: science could not inquire into natural laws of the origin of life, because that origin was divine in nature. The symbolic boundary was based on Scripture. Turner has argued that the reception of Darwin's theory owed much to the professionalization of science as a discipline and the change in attitudes to that discipline of the new generation of naturalists who were beginning to secure positions of power and responsibility (Turner, 1993). Increasing professionalization and popularization of science (Lightman, 1997; Turner, 1993) and the vested interests of the dominant class (Young, 1985), coupled with natural selection's appeal to a public sensitized to evolution (Desmond, 1989), helped secure a new symbolic boundary for the new inheritors of the imagined community – the boundary between those who believed in evolution and those who considered the matter was best left in God's hands. The promotion of biology to the accepted disciplines of the natural sciences was helped by the mathematization of the discipline. Darwin's grasp of statistics is basic, but his followers and heirs soon adopted rigorous statistical models from physics.

The ascent of the natural sciences was assured, and this is precisely what happened from the end of the nineteenth century right through the twentieth. They offered the truth and certainty about the material world (Lightman, 1997; Weinberg, 2015). They offered solutions to politicians and capitalists seeking to find advantages on the battlefield and in the workplace (Hobsbawm, 1989). They offered professional careers and professional validation through universities, degrees and published works (Turner, 1993). The natural sciences in the period of high modernity were seen as the 'handmaiden' of the modern, Western man, the bourgeois liberal who preferred to believe in the power of evolution to the power of Christ (Young, 1985). While in some countries, ruling elites and religious figures actively discouraged the spread of scientific ideas, in cities across the world middle-class reformers found science to be a normal and essential part of their worldview. Philosophers such as John Stuart Mill and Bertrand Russell rejected irrationality and promoted radical politics because of their belief in the veracity of the scientific tradition (Russell, 2013). The beauty of the scientific gaze was found in the tracks of particles in cloud chambers, or the carefully arranged models of organic chemistry, or maps of heredity.

DOI: 10.1057/9781137577917.0003

In the nineteenth century we see the first attempts to write social sciences in the manner of modern science. Darwin is wary of applying the theory of evolution to human culture and society, but others such as Galton and Spencer establish social Darwinism (Depew and Weber, 2011). These are natural scientists who take an interest in the social, and there are others, just as there are philosophers and social scientists such as James and Dewey who take an interest in natural sciences. This is the era in which politicians and other elites try to find ways in which they can improve societies, either through philanthropic morals or instrumental game-playing. The problem of the social world is theorized, and social sciences emerge as a normal part of science. The history of sociology and the social sciences in the nineteenth century and the early twentieth is too long to write, so I can only address a small part of it to get an idea of the trends (for sociology in the United Kingdom see Halsey, 2004). Comte, Marx and Durkheim attempt to construct a scientific sociology through radically different processes. Comte's sociology is explicitly quantitative and built on the idea that the only proper way to knowledge can be found in the methods of natural science (Gane, 2014; Heilbron, 2015; Inglis, 2014). Marx's sociology is a historical sociology drawing on philosophy and economics, which emerges almost as a by-product of his political theses (Blackledge, 2006; Kitching, 1988). Durkheim's sociology is more open to the idea that there are different kinds of sociological knowledge, and sociologists need to apply the right tools to the right problems if sociology and social science is to progress. For the founders of social sciences, there is a pressing need immediately to legitimate their sciences as proper sciences. Sociologists, psychologists and economists adopt the practices of the professional scientific community (Potter, 2014). And each of those three disciplines has debates about the problem with social sciences: the problem of doing controlled and replicable experiments on the social world. Almost as soon as social sciences are formed and legitimized, then, they are strongly criticized by natural scientists and by those within social science, because they are unable to produce true and certain answers, because they are unable to construct theories that can be tested in controlled experiments (ibid.). For psychology, the answer is to become just like a natural science. For economics, the answer is to create abstract models. For sociology, the answer remains unresolved to this day.

DOI: 10.1057/9781137577917.0003

Discussion: science today – big science, STEM and social sciences

Since the middle of the past century, when the Cold War poured billions of dollars into research and development, modern science has become big science, an industry funded partly by trans-national corporations seeking profits from patents, and national governments seeking military and economic hegemony (Fuller, 2000a, 2000b; Galison and Hevly, 1992; Latour, 1987). The era of late modernity that coincided with the Cold War saw the reputation of science soar in the public imagination, in popular culture and in policy-making circles. Science fiction stories showed that humans would find paradize on earth through the technologies science would provide and paradizes in new worlds. As scientists designed and built the technologies that took humans into space and to the moon, it seemed that science could do no wrong. As universities in the global North started to open up their intake to a wider demographic intake of students, natural science and engineering courses became seen as the best ways in which nation-states could build stronger economies and futures (Woolgar, 1988). Private corporations stared to invest in university laboratories to get commissioned research on projects that helped them gain market advantage, and the biggest corporations bought their own research labs and scientists, who were hired to work for the interests of those corporations (Fuller, 2000a, 2000b; Latour, 1987; Woolgar, 1981). At the same time, social sciences were seen as an integral part of the scientific enterprise and were given support by nation-states and corporations in a similar way to the natural sciences. In the television series *Star Trek*, for example, we see scientist members of the crew who are said to be sociologists or psychologists.

The growing crises of the environment – global warming, the widening hole in the ozone layer, species extinction, pollution and the problem of nuclear power – led from the 1960s onwards to a shift in the public mood about science and scientists. From thinking scientists were clever folks in white lab-coats, the lab-coat itself became emblematic of the malevolence and carelessness of the modern scientist (Haraway, 1987; Latour, 1987). When Star Trek invented itself as *The Next Generation* in the 1980s, the danger of the single-minded scientists causing disaster to the people and world around him or her is addressed in a number of episodes, even though the future Earth envisaged has used science to solve its problems. In some radical left-wing circles, modern science was

DOI: 10.1057/9781137577917.0003

seen as a cause of environmental and social problems, a tool of capitalism and patriarchy, which despoiled the world without caring about the consequences. Some academics in the social sciences started to distance their work from that of the natural sciences, and by the 1990s there was a clear trend in sociology where radical and/or feminist researchers eschewed quantitative methods, which turned humans into data, for 'rich' ethnographic or qualitative sociology (Guba and Lincoln, 1989; Lincoln and Guba, 1985). Feminist and post-structural epistemologies were written that rejected scientism, the myth of objectivity and the idea of progress, for the exploration of power and meaning (Haraway, 1989). Sociology is still dominated by such work.

This period of late modernity, up to the end of the 1960s, also saw the works of historians of science such as Thomas Kuhn (1957, 1962) become known in the popular imagination. Kuhn's work seemed to suggest that the cumulative growth of science was not correct, and that science operated through paradigmatic change. Kuhn, as Fuller (2000b) claims in his biography of him, is known more by reputation – the reputation of his 1962 book *The Structure of Scientific Revolution* – than by encounter. Fuller's main argument is that Kuhn's book, rather than being the radical break with positivism and the text for a relativized world, is actually a normative, theoretically conservative project undertaken to justify the autonomy of science in post-war America. Fuller argues that to understand Kuhn we have to place Kuhn in his context. Kuhn was a product of Harvard and an acolyte of Conant, who believed in the autonomy of science and was fighting, after the end of the Second World War, to keep research inside universities and to translate the model of Big Science to the campus. This was, claims Fuller, part of Conant's project to defend the spirit of science, interpreted in the light of the Cold War and Conant's anti-communist politics, against totalitarianism. Teaching, and in particular the curriculum at Harvard, was crucial to the success of this project. At this point in the story, Kuhn appears as the man with the model of science that fits neatly into the Conant project. According to Fuller, Kuhn belonged to a generation of physicists disillusioned by the appropriation of science to military ends during the war. Because of this disillusionment, Kuhn turned to the history and philosophy of science – according to Fuller, a discipline that at the time did not exist institutionally – to try to construct a normative natural philosophy by rational means. This was the motivation for Kuhn to write *Structure*.

DOI: 10.1057/9781137577917.0003

Fuller shows that Kuhn wrote Structure with a narrow evidence base for the model: European physics from 1620 to 1920. This narrow base, claims Fuller, was a deliberate attempt to demarcate normal science and to provide a normative model of what knowledge is. So, according to Fuller, this would appear to undermine the use made by the social sciences of Kuhn to legitimize their own practices, a move disapproved of by Kuhn himself. For Fuller, this move puts Kuhn firmly in the camp of the positivists, who were trying to construct such normative models based on narrow definitions of science and drawing upon exemplars from the history of science. In this sense, Kuhn was not a historian but a normative, historicist philosopher trying to elucidate the best practice of gaining knowledge. According to Fuller, Kuhn was only interested in knowledge, unlike Popper (2005), Polanyi (1958) and Feyerabend (1975) who used their normative models of science to engage with these wider issues. Fuller argues that this lack of responsiveness in Kuhn was due to Kuhn's sheltered background and his close relationship with Conant and others at Harvard who looked after him and made sure his career went smooth, despite his failure to get tenure.

As someone who was a child in the shadow of the Cold War in the 1970s and 1980s, I found natural sciences presented all around me as a way to truth about the world, and also as a way of making the world a better place. I read comics and watched programmes on television that told me how science had eclipsed religion and shown humanity the truth about ourselves. We were not sacred beings: we were animals, molecules thrown together by the passing of billions of years of time. We were not at the centre of the universe. Like Kuhn, I saw beauty in the truth and methods of natural science, and decided early on in life I wanted to be a physicist. As I came to my A-Levels I decided I preferred chemistry, and did Natural Sciences at the start of the 1990s at Cambridge, where I had the joy of studying both. With other 'NatScis' around me, we made fun of the people doing social and political sciences, because all they did was read books and have a couple of lectures, while we sweated away at titration and mass-spectrometry analysis. Although I later crossed over to the humanities and social sciences, I was like so many others a child of the positivists in science. I was a scientist, and believed academic disciplines that did not look like physics or chemistry were not proper sciences. I went into physics and chemistry because they were the exciting subjects that gave all the answers, which pointed to a future of space travel and the end of religion. I knew that there was a left-wing radical

DOI: 10.1057/9781137577917.0003

critique of science, and I shared the concerns from the Green Movement about the problems caused by pollution. But I believed that only science could solve the problems caused by global capitalism and military struggle. I had seen the huge advances made in medicine, and knew this was made possible by open science, the public sphere of testing and finding out causes (Popper, 2005).

My teenage prejudices were not peculiar to Britain at the end of the past century. But, in fact, the prejudice I had is now still common place in the popular imagination. If we want to know how the sciences, natural and social, have fared in our time, in this century, we need look no further than the hugely popular American television programme *The Big Bang Theory*. The sit-com revolves around two scientists who share a flat: Sheldon and Leonard (Bednarek, 2012). They are typical caricatures of the modern nerd: they hang out at the comic-book store, watch and adore Star Wars and Star Trek and eat take-way food. While Leonard is human enough to have love interests, Sheldon borders on some form of Asperger's syndrome. *The Big Bang Theory* shows us, first, that the idea of science as a vocation, and as a pursuit of truth, is an acceptable backdrop to a Hollywood show. Sheldon and Leonard do their physics in full view of the audience, whether it is Sheldon's whiteboard in their flat, or Leonard's laboratory on the campus. The makers of the show ensure that the science is as accurate as possible, and drop in gags that only people who know physics and chemistry can understand. They portray a life of science where researchers pursue and receive funding, and publish extensively, in their struggle to gain tenure. Sheldon may be an asexual geek who embodies the American high-school myth of clever science kids, but Leonard is normal enough to have a tall, blonde-haired cheerleader-type woman for a girlfriend. What Leonard, Sheldon and the other scientists do is portrayed as cool and defended as a way of showing us a better future, even if there are hierarchies within science that mean Howard, with no PhD and specialism in engineering, is looked down on by Sheldon. And this leads to the second thing that *The Big Bang Theory* tells us about science, loosely defined: the social sciences are seen as less important in the wider academic industry, and in the public imagination. Sheldon is the voice of the STEM industry when he dismisses anything that is not a natural science. In the episode 'The Benefactor Factor' (Series 4, Episode 15), the scientists are instructed by their manager to attend an event where they talk to the potential funders of research. At first Sheldon is reluctant to go, but his 'girlfriend' Amy says:

DOI: 10.1057/9781137577917.0003

Well then, prepare to be terrified. If your friends are unconvincing, this year's donations might go to, say, the Geology department.

Sheldon: Oh no. Not the dirt people!
Amy: Or, worse still, it could go to the liberal arts.
Sheldon: No!
Amy: Millions of dollars being showered on poets, literary theorists and students of gender studies.
Sheldon: Oh, the humanities!

In another episode ('The Friendship Algorithm', Series 2 Episode 13), Sheldon observes that the social sciences are mostly 'hokum'. Sheldon may be a comically funny caricature of the insecure, theoretical physicist, but his defence of physics as proper science and everything else as degrees of 'hokum' (all the way down to the humanities) is only what many politicians, policy-makers and writers in the public sphere think; social sciences are not proper sciences if they do not use the mathematical and epistemological tools of natural science (Flyvbjerg, 2001).

The cause of natural sciences in popular culture is propagated too by the growing number of blogs, magazines and books that tell their readers about how amazing proper science is. It is not unusual to see popular science books in the bestseller charts for non-fiction books (Harari, 2015; Kahneman, 2011). Even where the social sciences might be involved, such as with Kahneman's (2011) book on psychology, these books are always weighted down with reference to experimental design, data and testing. This rise in interest in natural science, and social science that masquerades as natural science, is associated with the more assertive secularism promoted by the New Atheists, which in turn is associated strongly with the scientist turned popular science writer Richard Dawkins (2006). This movement started out defending science, especially the theory of evolution, through natural selection, from religious critics seeking to defend their own beliefs about creation (Dennett, 2006). Dawkins's early books specifically engage with the pseudo-science of creationism, revealing it to be a nonsense with no intellectual weight to it (Dawkins, 1986). Latterly, New Atheism has become more muscular, especially since the attacks by Islamic terrorists in 2001 on America, and the subsequent focus in the media on the struggle between a supposedly secular West and an Islamic East (Hitchens, 2007). For the New Atheists, their defence of science becomes a way of raising the gates against the fundamentalist Other, especially the Islamist ideologies (Harris, 2004; Dawkins, 2006).

DOI: 10.1057/9781137577917.0003

STEM has become a shorthand for the natural sciences, even though it might be argued that the social sciences are a sub-set of the science in STEM. But the logic of STEM is to exclude the social sciences – STEM means the important sciences, the popular ones, the natural sciences. Psychology might be included in the sciences if it demonstrates its methods and thinking equates to the natural science epistemological traditions – if it can demonstrate its commitment to finding out the truth through controlled experiments, and if it shows impact on policy and profits for industry (Fuller, 2000a). In university funding, STEM courses and modules receive extra resources from governments and other funding bodies (Gough, 2014). In government policies, STEM is seen as an important sector of the economy, and many governments place higher education into departments of business, because STEM is about making money. Supporting the STEM industry means favouring STEM teaching in universities and STEM research in funding decisions. STEM teaching means training the lab workers of the future, highly skilled but mobile individuals who will move from project to project, from university to corporation, finding things out and making money. STEM thinking, as Ben Goldacre (2008) argues, is actually bad science, because it has privatized the search for knowledge – this means, for instance, that most research on new medicines is funded by pharmaceutical companies, who keep much of the findings unpublished (Goldacre, 2014). But campaigns against the rise of STEM thinking are not as vocal in the public sphere than campaigns promoting STEM. The dominance of STEM thinking can be found in the prevalence of STEM campaigns in the public sphere, and STEM policies in governments across the world. In the United Kingdom, we have the Campaign for Science and Engineering and Science Matters, a campaign run by the British Science Association to ensure people engage with and understand science (http://www.britishscienceassociation.org/science-matters). Science Matters uses carefully worded statements about 'conversations' about the importance of science, but it is clear that its aim is to get people to abandon any scepticism they might have about the economic and moral importance of STEM and STEM funding and education. The Campaign for Science and Engineering is a lobbying group with close connections to politicians, civil servants and journalists. It says:

> Our mission is to raise the political profile of science and engineering. We passionately believe in the economic and cultural importance of scientific and technological education and development, and the vital need for the funding

of this research by Government and industry. (http://sciencecampaign.org. uk/?page_id=5394, accessed 31 August 2015)

On its pages, it provides press releases and policy briefings that argue the economic value of STEM subjects and the importance of STEM education:

> Science and engineering lie at the heart of our economy, so ensuring Britain has a skilled STEM workforce is essential. We campaign for the highest quality and most effective teaching structures at all stages of education. (http://sciencecampaign.org.uk/?tag=stem-education, accessed 31 August 2015)

It is instructive to read the political party manifestos and policy papers for what they tell us about the acceptance in the public sphere of STEM thinking, and the influence of the messages about STEM from the campaigns and the industry itself. All three main political parties in England (Labour, the Conservatives and the Liberal Democrats) promise to protect and promote science education and the STEM industry. They all promise investment in STEM because it is vital to the economy. The Conservative Party, who were the major coalition partner in the previous government, and who won the 2015 General Election, say:

> Great science is worthwhile in its own right and yields enormous practical benefits too – curing diseases, driving technological innovation, promoting business investment and informing public policy for the better. We ringfenced the science budget by making difficult choices to reduce spending in other areas. Now we will invest new capital on a record scale – £6.9 billion in the UK's research infrastructure up to 2021 – which will mean new equipment, new laboratories and new research institutes. (Conservative Party, 2015, p. 23)

From this extract from the Conservative Party manifesto it is clear what it thinks science is: it is the big science of big technology and resources. The Conservatives believe that research should be directed towards STEM, the hard sciences or the natural sciences – because these are the ones that cure disease, make profits and help boost the technology industries. Only the fourth practical benefit listed might be something that the social sciences might be able to address, and this is the last benefit listed, almost as a red-faced afterthought. What better public policy might mean is of course helping the government find answers to its problems, not to make the world a better place. This is the discourse of impact. The admission that great science is worthwhile in its own right is interesting. The key words are 'great' and 'yields', that is, science is worthwhile in its own right as long as it yields those practical benefits.

DOI: 10.1057/9781137577917.0003

And that is the science the Conservatives will fund: STEM research that yields economic and political impacts and benefits.

The United Kingdom Independence Party (UKIP) is a radical, right-wing populist party, with many similarities to the Tea Party in the United States, though it is a separately constituted party that competes against the Conservatives (Ford and Goodwin, 2014). Although it has struggled to gain seats in Parliament, it won a significant share of the vote in the 2015 General Election (12.6 per cent), and won the most seats in Britain in the previous year's European Elections. It is true to say that UKIP has altered the political centre of Britain, shifting it rightwards. In its 2015 Manifesto, it promises:

> Waive tuition fees for students taking a degree in science; technology; engineering; maths or medicine. (UKIP, 2015, p. 5)

This commitment is so important to UKIP that it appears in the introduction to its manifesto, as well as under its section on education and small businesses. UKIP believes that the way to improve the UK's economy and world position is to invest in STEM teaching and training. By waiving the fee on STEM subjects it is hoping that students will choose those courses instead of going on the social sciences or the humanities. It is Sheldon Cooper's cry all over again. Further on, it stresses its commitment to get more natural science education, name-checking and endorsing one of the pressure groups promoting STEM subjects:

> To increase the uptake of science learning at secondary level, we will follow the recommendations of the Campaign for Science and Engineering and require every primary school to nominate (and train, if necessary) a science leader to inspire and equip the next generation. (UKIP, 2015, p. 29)

UKIP's policy favours STEM over the social sciences and humanities and shows that they are tapping into a mood in the public sphere that the social sciences are not proper sciences. UKIP may be seen as an opportunist, right-wing fringe party, but they are only saying what others are thinking: the social sciences should not be treated the same as the natural sciences, and natural sciences should be privileged over the social sciences when it comes to policy and funding decisions. This debate is not confined to the United Kingdom, either. In the United States of America, campaigns promoting natural sciences have been backed by senior politicians, who have also attracted social sciences and humanities in the same reports that they boast the value of the natural sciences:

> Last fall a task force organized by Gov. Rick Scott of Florida caused a national outcry with the recommendation that state universities charge higher tuition to students in fields – like anthropology or English – deemed less likely to lead to jobs. At the same time, Republicans in Congress have repeatedly tried to eliminate financing for political science research through the National Science Foundation, except for that deemed to be essential for national security. (http://www.nytimes.com/2013/06/19/arts/humanities-committee-sounds-an-alarm.html?_r=0, accessed 31 August 2015)

These kinds of attacks happen because the social sciences are perceived to be less scientific, that is, less robust in their epistemological and methodological rigour. But they are also seen as having less economic benefit, too. These two problems people have with social science cannot be separated out – the lack of confidence in the social sciences predicting the future is the reason why its findings are not useful to the instrumental logic of capitalism or government bureaucracies.

Research Councils UK (RCUK) is the lead organization to which every government-funded research council in the United Kingdom belongs. It has driven the push across all the research councils to ensure that every application to them includes statements about pathways to impact: academic and what it calls 'economic and societal'. Each research council makes it clear that failing to demonstrate such impacts means applications for funding will be rejected. All the projects that are funded therefore show clear 'pathways' to making those impacts. Academic impact is straightforward enough. The other form of impact is more problematic to demonstrate, though it is easy to define. According to RCUK,

> Economic and societal impacts embrace all the extremely diverse ways in which research-related knowledge and skills benefit individuals, organisations and nations by: fostering global economic performance, and specifically the economic competitiveness of the United Kingdom; increasing the effectiveness of public services and policy; enhancing quality of life, health and creative output. (http://www.rcuk.ac.uk/innovation/impacts/, accessed 20 August 2015)

The Economic and Social Research Council (ESRC) is the funding council that supports social science research in the United Kingdom. It added the 'economic' to its original name (social science research council) under the right-wing Tory government of Margaret Thatcher, who

DOI: 10.1057/9781137577917.0003

wanted the council to fund research that was more of a public concern, that is, research that would help the government help businesses. The ESRC says:

> Determining the impact of social science research is not a straightforward task. Policy and service development is not a linear process, and decisions are rarely taken on the basis of research evidence alone. This makes it difficult to pin down the role that an individual piece of research has played. The timing of evaluation also presents challenges. Too soon after the research ends may mean that any impact has yet to fully develop. Too late, and the impact may no longer be traceable as people involved have moved on. (http://www.esrc. ac.uk/funding-and-guidance/impact-toolkit/what-how-and-why/what-is-research-impact.aspx, accessed 20 August 2015)

This advice to social science researchers is sound. It is not straight-forward to show the economic and societal impact of any social science research. To try to do that one needs to show that one's research clearly falls under the definitions of such impact used by the RCUK. How does social science show it has contributed in a significant way to global capitalism and the Gross Domestic Product (GDP) of a nation-state's economy? It can only do it by compromising its methods and ethics, so that it produces research that looks like the natural sciences, in terms of experimental design, testability and profitability. How does social science show that it can inform policy? It can do that only by producing find-ings that politicians and civil servants understand, so it has to follow the epistemological logic of the natural sciences and come up with simple and straightforward answers or recommendations. And how does social science show that it improves quality of life? Actually, it does. Everything researched in the social sciences improves our humanity and the qual-ity of our lives. But is that measurable? In the next chapter, I am going to return to these themes, because they form the basis of campaigns defending the social sciences.

The state of social sciences today, then, is an uncertain one. As I will show in the next chapter, there are social sciences courses and schools in universities around the world. There are social sciences in school curricula, though these are increasingly being squeezed out in favour of core subjects such as natural sciences and maths. There are learned societies for all the social sciences, and a healthy range of subject fields underpinned by the social sciences, such as my own (leisure studies). There are still thousands of us around the world debating social science theory and doing social science research. But the social sciences are

DOI: 10.1057/9781137577917.0003

feeling the pinch when it comes to research funding, funding for student places, and prestige in popular culture and the public sphere. Despite a certain suspicion about science in contemporary popular culture that has survived from the Green Movement, and the denial of scientific knowledge on the fringes of far-right politics (such as those who deny that climate change is happening and say it is a conspiracy by scientists and the United Nations to stop Americans being free – see McCright and Dunlap, 2011), the natural sciences retain a privileged place in the ways of thinking and the ways of legitimizing knowledge and power in the modern world. STEM thinking makes as common-sense truth the contested claim that all human experience can be reduced to its economic value, and everything social can be reduced to the natural or discarded as false knowledge.

DOI: 10.1057/9781137577917.0003

2
The Weakness of the Defence

Abstract: *Spracklen shows the weakness of the defence made by social scientists today ad historically, which are dominated by instrumental ways of thinking about the value of the work. The social sciences have been enthralled by two related ideas – the idea that the social might be measured by a slide-rule or computer; and the idea that the social sciences might be a tool to make governments work efficiently and industries make bigger profits. If social sciences make the case for their work and existence by measuring impact, measuring income-generation and fetishizing scientific methods, they allow themselves to be the subject of reduction to the 'big' natural sciences, and allow themselves to be subsumed.*

Spracklen, Karl. *Making the Moral Case for Social Sciences: Stemming the Tide.* Basingstoke: Palgrave Macmillan, 2016. DOI: 10.1057/9781137577917.0004.

DOI: 10.1057/9781137577917.0004

This chapter begins by setting out some of the more publicly argued responses or defences made by people about the legitimacy of the social sciences. I then turn to arguments made historically about the instrumental value of the social sciences in the West, from the period of High Modernity in the late nineteenth century to the positivist turns in the second half of the twentieth century. I show that the social sciences have been enthralled by two related ideas – the idea that the social might be measured by a slide-rule or computer; and the idea that the social sciences might be a tool to make governments work efficiently and industries make bigger profits. In the second half of the chapter the cases of economics, psychology and sociology will be explored and critiqued in more detail. I show that economics is the moral exemplar of an over-confidence in scientific rhetoric and methods. I show that the recent history of psychology is accommodation with natural sciences and the reductionist assumptions that the social can easily be explained as something natural, and something simple that can be monetized. I will show that sociology has faced similar pressures to follow the twin pressures of scientism and neo-liberalism. In the concluding section of the chapter I will show that the regimes of global capitalism, hegemony and governmentality that have taken over universities, education and government planning make the attempt to emulate STEM thinking in social sciences only serve to legitimize the instrumentality at the heart of this takeover. If social sciences make the case for their work and existence by measuring impact, measuring income-generation and fetishizing scientific methods, they allow themselves to be the subject of reduction to the 'big' natural sciences, and allow themselves to be subsumed.

Defending social sciences today

There are many people who have written or otherwise have made positive noises about the importance of the social sciences in contemporary society (see, e.g., the important contributions in Bastow, Dunleavy and Tinkler, 2014; Lynd, 2015). Social scientists make the case every day in our working lives, whether we are involved in research or teaching a first-year class. I am aware of the thousands of voices of such campaigners and enthusiasts, from the people like Giddens and Bauman writing books that every sociology student reads, right through to my colleagues justifying their social science research every day of their working lives.

DOI: 10.1057/9781137577917.0004

I am a member of quite a number of learned societies that make such cases in their aims and in their conferences and publications. But this advocacy work is strongest inside classrooms, and inside or between higher education establishments. In the public sphere, such advocacy work is generally limited to liberal newspapers interviewing social scientists, or social scientists writing letters to liberal newspapers. Where are the social sciences equivalents of campaigns such as the Campaign for Science and Engineering, and what are they saying? They do exist. But they are not making the right case for the social sciences.

The Campaign for Social Science is the most important and highest-profile campaigning group promoting the social sciences in the United Kingdom. It is has been set up by the Academy of Social Sciences, a national organization analogous to the various academies or societies of science that exist around the world. The Academy has the learned societies of most social sciences and related subject fields as its members: for example, the British Sociological Association are members, as well as the British Psychological Society. In addition to learned societies as members, it elects individuals as academicians who have an important reputation. Its academicians are world-class scholars and other workers in the social sciences. The Campaign for Social Science has the financial and moral support of many of the learned societies, as well as academic publishers such as Palgrave and Sage. In February 2015 it launched a key state-of-the-science report ahead of the British General Election. It is necessary to report in full the story as reported in the news release on the campaign's website. But my analysis will break the up the new release into its sections. Instead of making the case for social sciences, the report is reduced in the headline and the opening paragraph to a plea for more money:

> *Social scientists urge 10 per cent uplift in budget for science and innovation*
>
> February 24, 2015
>
> The £4.7 billion annual budget for science and innovation should increase by at least 10 per cent in real terms over the next parliament, the Campaign for Social Science says in a report on the prospects for social science over the next decade. At the launch of the report on 24 February, Greg Clark MP, Minister for Universities, Science and Cities, talked about the value of social science. *The Business of People: The Significance of Social Science over the Next Decade* also calls for a new senior Whitehall social science adviser, more investment in Big Data, social science advice for MPs and members of the devolved administrations and more explicit recognition for social science

DOI: 10.1057/9781137577917.0004

in government strategy. It says additional funds for science and innovation should be earmarked for research that brings together the perspectives of the physical and life sciences with those from social science, the arts and humanities.

(https://campaignforsocialscience.org.uk/news/social-scientists-urge-10-per-cent-uplift-budget-science-innovation/, accessed 24 August 2015)

As the opening paragraph, this is the most important part of the story about the report. And what does it say? The social sciences need more money, but they should get more money only by working collaboratively with the natural sciences on the innovation UK PLC needs to succeed. Note that the title of the report even fetishizes the word business. This is what social scientists are apparently doing – we are the business, the industry, of people. We have been reduced to marketing managers. The news release continues this theme. The only important value the social sciences have is the instrumental one they can give to the government and the industry:

> The report warns that UK growth and prosperity will falter without a better grasp of human behaviour and public attitudes, especially in the service sector of the economy. Failing to understand the socio-economic dimensions of innovation could jeopardise the potential of new technologies and advances in the life sciences, physics and engineering. The report gives the recent example of Ebola and infectious disease, which can only be combatted through understanding people and communities. (Ibid.)

Of course this is all true. Managers and policy-makers do need insights and understanding from the social sciences to run the economy more efficiently, especially as we are now in a post-Fordist, post-industrial, global and mobile economy (Urry, 2003, 2007). Natural scientists need our insights and understanding if they are to understand the impacts of their technologies and the limits of their models. But the news release gives the social sciences a secondary role to natural sciences and global capitalism. The purpose of social sciences is to help the natural scientists get more truthful assessments of their problems, and to help inform the transformation of natural science knowledge into a more profitable and managerialist world. There is in the report more nuanced defences of the social sciences, but the news release serves to distil the complexities in the report into the things the campaign thinks politicians and the public sphere need to hear. This paragraph should make the moral case for social sciences above and beyond the reductionist logic of the free market and

DOI: 10.1057/9781137577917.0004

policy impact. But it does not. It says the only important thing about the social sciences is the contribution they sometimes make to the instrumental goals of (post-)modern government and (post-)modern global capital. The report continues with three sound-bites from influential people, including the head of the ESRC and the chair of the campaign:

> Professor Jane Elliott, chief executive of the Economic & Social Research Council, another speaker at the launch event, said: 'Social science is vital to a vibrant and fair society. The UK's world-class research enables us to better understand our communities, institutions and economy. The impact it has is extremely valuable in both human and economic terms.'

> Campaign chair Professor James Wilsdon said: 'Whatever the outcome of the general election, the challenges facing the UK demand the skills, insights and imagination of social scientists. Growth, health, security and wellbeing all depend on knowing how markets, organisations, individuals and households work, making investment in social science a critical component of the government's strategy for science and innovation. It's with confidence in the absolute necessity of social science that this report stakes its claim on scarce resources.'

> Dr Michelle Harrison, Global Head of Social and Political Practice at TNS and a member of the report working group, noted that 'Across many areas of public policy, and increasingly in the world's leading corporations, we are seeing the increasing adoption of approaches that are at the heart of social science thinking, to tackle some of our biggest problems, whether they be to do with issues of governance or of corporate growth. Behavioural insight is one example, where social science is key to understanding how to communicate with citizens and consumers, and to encourage behaviour change for a better social outcome.'

Jane Elliott from the ESRC starts with a moral argument about fairness and vibrancy, which should be central to how the ESRC understands the impact of the social sciences, but still returns to the economy. James Wilsdon from the campaign is almost completely instrumental: this is about the value of the social sciences to the government, to natural sciences and to the economy. Michelle Harrison from TNS, a 'global research agency' dedicated to helping governments and corporations make better financial and policy decisions through better data, is unsurprisingly more instrumental. The news release on the report ends with a call for a chief social scientist, who would help the government make profit and policy:

> The report urges the appointment of a chief social science adviser to work alongside Sir Mark Walport, the government chief scientific adviser, to ensure better mobilisation of knowledge for policymakers and oversee the pipeline of graduate students in vital areas of social science, moving into

DOI: 10.1057/9781137577917.0004

business and research. Whitehall departments, along with the Westminster parliament and devolved institutions, must make more intensive use of social science in the years ahead if they are to cope with pressing questions around cities, transport, political alienation, social mobility, energy, health and wellbeing and climate change. R&D tax relief must recognise innovations in the way companies and public sector organisations work derived from social science expertise. Professor Wilsdon added: 'At the election and during the spending review that will follow, the Campaign has a robust case to make to the Treasury, ministers, MPs and policymakers. Support for research, data collection and education and training in social science are vital if we are to secure the benefits of innovation and productivity growth. Without more investment in social science, the UK will lose out'. (Ibid.)

Inside the report itself, this economic and policy impact is spelled out even more clearly than in the news release. What we see in the pages of the report is the adoption of the language of modern government, where the aim of governing is to manage resources efficiently, and to allow the free market to operate (Bruff, 2014; Dawson, 2013; Docherty, 2015; Jones, 2014). This neo-liberal ideology places faith in the market for solutions to problems through the reification of innovation and the entrepreneur (Jones, 2014). In the modern, global world in which we live, such innovation naturally comes from the world of digital technology and the service sectors (Urry, 2007). In both of these areas of the post-industrial society, natural science is seen as both a font of wisdom and a source of justification for practice. So the social sciences are presented as being in partnership with the natural sciences in helping the wheel of government, and the wheel of finance, turn. Science feeds capitalism, capitalism feeds science. The report states:

> Advancing and applying science depends on profits, policies, markets, organisations and attitudes. These are social science themes. In *Our plan for growth* (the science and innovation strategy published in December 2014), the government underlined the necessity of deploying 'all the sciences'. Within this mix, social science supplies tools, concepts and models to help us think about and run the state and markets. We join with colleagues from other disciplines in calling for more public investment in research. The advance of knowledge is a precondition for prosperity (and the tax revenues it supplies). (Campaign for Social Science, 2015, p. xi)

Here the campaign aligns itself with existing government policies for the sciences, which see them as a key driver in the growth of the economy. Natural sciences, as we have seen in the previous chapter, are seen by

DOI: 10.1057/9781137577917.0004

policy-makers as being essential for growth, because their epistemology creates confidence in knowledge-claims and predictions, which in turn create confidence in markets and economies. Social sciences are thrown into this instrumental purpose. It is social sciences knowledge that can help the government and its officials run the free market. The final parenthesis is a depressing one for a report written by a campaign for social sciences. Is the audience of policy-makers, politicians and journalists who are being encouraged to read this report too stupid to understand this claim without it being spelled out in simple terms? And are social scientists too naïve to write such a statement, when we know full well that modern governments work closely with trans-national corporations to actively reduce tax revenues (Jones, 2014)? In addition to telling its readers that the social sciences are a source of economic value, a benefit to industry so long as they are working alongside the natural sciences, the report makes a second big claim: it argues that social sciences are important for the better management of government. As such, it argues that social science education and training and development needs to be transformed. This might be viewed as a good thing for the social sciences, but already the kinds of social science that 'matter' are reduced to the quantitative and analytical ones that resemble the natural sciences. In making this case the report takes a moment to criticize social science teachers for being rubbish at teaching their students things other than number-crunching skills:

> Within Whitehall, cross-government thinking about demands for evidence and analysis should extend to training, data and international research collaboration. Supply is a pressing theme. Social science students extend the talent pool for data analysis and interpretation. Improving their quantitative and analytic skills is a task for the universities, learned societies, national academies, the Department for Education (DfE), the Department for Business, Innovation and Skills (BIS), the devolved administrations and the Nuffield Foundation (which has instigated the Q-Step programme, supported by the ESRC and the higher education funding councils). Loans for taught master's degrees, agreed by the coalition government, must ensure fair access across the social sciences. Social science expertise is needed to evaluate costs and the effects of the policy on, for example, social mobility and earnings and in meeting strategic needs. (ibid, p. 4)

With defences such as this one, social sciences and their practitioners are made to feel their work is worthless. We are caught between the Scylla of not being scientific enough, and the Charybdis of not making enough money for the economy.

Defending social sciences in modernity

The arguments made defending social sciences today echo similar arguments made historically about the instrumental value of the social sciences in the West, from the period of High Modernity in the late nineteenth century to the positivist, or rather, quantitative turns in the second half of the twentieth century. Just as the Campaign for Social Science tells the public sphere that the social sciences are important because they help the economy and the rational logic of government, the founders and popularizers of the social sciences said exactly the same thing. Auguste Comte, for example, believed sociology to be the science of society, a way of making modern humans understand the best way to govern, and the best way to live (Comte, 1868). This science of society would help society prosper through creating the optimal conditions in which scientific progress could operate to create increased wealth and increased power for the nations of the West. Comte's sociology was essentially utopian, promising hegemonic elites a way of increasing their power and wealth while increasing divisions in labour and between classes (Ekelund Jr and Olsen, 1973; Heilbron, 2015). Comte's idea of a social science epistemology – if not the positivist details – was adopted by those who came after him who saw an instrumental role for the science of society in making modern, nineteenth-century society. Herbert Spencer was the most popular social science author in this period, an acolyte of Galton and the social Darwinists (Claeys, 2000; Hawkins, 1997). Like Galton, Spencer wrote books that showed their middle-class, bourgeois readers a glimpse of the new and exciting science of society (Duncan, 2013). In the defence of social sciences, Spencer begins by showing his readers that the social sciences are important because they will solve the problems faced by every politician, the problems of how to make the right decisions to improve the commonwealth of the nation:

> Over his pipe in the village ale-house, the labourer says very positively what Parliament should do about the 'foot and mouth disease'. At the farmer's market-table his master makes the glasses jingle as, with his fist, he emphasizes the assertion that he did not get half enough compensation for his slaughtered beasts during the cattle-plague. These are not hesitating opinions. On a matter affecting the agricultural interest, it is still as it was during the Anti-Corn-Law agitation, when, in every rural circle, you heard that the nation would be ruined if the lightly-taxed foreigner was allowed to compete in our markets with the heavily-taxed Englishman: a proposition

DOI: 10.1057/9781137577917.0004

held to be so self-evident that dissent from it implied either stupidity or knavery. (Spencer, 1873, p. 1)

The examples provided show us what Spencer thought were the typical problems of his age, and ones that would be understood by his readers. The problem of agrarian reform dominated the minds of everyone from politicians and philosophers to the farmers and labourers who needed work, and the workers in the cities who needed to be fed. Spencer is already clear in this first paragraph that he is dismissive of those who stand against the free import of food into the country. The application of social science epistemology leads him to this conclusion later in the book, so we are treated in this first paragraph to false opinions, things he shows us to be prejudices through his use of the caricatures and stereotypes: the smoking labourer, the fist-wielding farmer. The farmers say people who do not try to stop free trade of corn are 'stupid or knaves', but Spencer wants to show us that it is they who are the stupid knaves. And just as the 'common man' is wrong in his prejudices against free trade, he is wrong to demand so much intervention from government. These knaves allow prejudice to shape their opinions rather than the instrumental logic of the social sciences, which points towards free trade and markets for the optimal solutions. Spencer was a radical free-market liberal who applied his beliefs about biology and the evolutionary notion of the 'survival of the fittest' to his social science. The success of the British Empire and the rise of America depended on the freedom given to individuals to make money from capitalist speculation and industry (Desmond, 1989; Hobsbawm, 1988, 1989). He believed that the role of government was to interfere as little as possible in the market, and that his scientific inquiry demanded such a *laissez-faire* economy. Spencer's case for the social sciences, then, was linked to his political views about the supremacy of the West and the importance of small government and free trade: he argued that social sciences allowed him to demonstrate the efficacy of those views.

But it was not just populist right-wing authors who argued that the value of the social sciences was an instrumental one. John Stuart Mill suggested that sociology was the key science that underpinned all social scientific inquiry, and all social scientific inquiry would help politicians see the utility or not of things such as free markets, progressive taxtaion and liberal democracy (Brink, 1992; Capaldi, 2004). His idea that good modern government demanded the appliance of social science was

DOI: 10.1057/9781137577917.0004

taken up by reformers in nation-states around the world. Modern liberal governments came to be dominated by rationalized bureaucracies, as Habermas (1984, 1987, 1989) and Weber (1992) both show, in which civil servants and politicians alike were trained in statistics and the social sciences of economic and sociology so that they would be able to make policy based on evidence, and make economic plans to create prosperity and political hegemony (Gramsci, 1971). In this stage of high modernity, the social sciences were eventually demarcated as being separate from the natural sciences in epistemological and ontological terms (as first argued at the turn of the twentieth century by the German philosopher Wilhelm Dilthey, 1989), but even so, the social sciences were presented as instrumental processes for better and more profitable government planning. The social sciences explained why society was structured in the way it was, but also gave modern policy-makers the means to test and explore the best ways to make society. That is, the social sciences were sources of knowledge that somehow increased prosperity, as well as test-sites of new ways of shaping the public and the political (Gramsci, 1971; Weber, 1992). Even Marx argued for the instrumental value of sociology and by extension social science (Alexander, 2014; Lefebvre, 1982).

The founding figure of modern sociology, Emile Durkheim, is instructive for this chapter's argument. Durkheim's influence on sociology does not need much further comment here. He is the most influential defender of sociology in its formative period, and is still one of the biggest influences on modern sociological theory and methods, so much so that his work is often cited in the present tense and not in the historical past tense. Durkheim believed that sociology could be a distinct social science with an ontology of social facts and an epistemology of scientific statistical methods, using such tools to construct theories, explanations and predictions of the social world. In *The Rule of Sociological Method* Durkheim (1982) wrote a history and philosophy of sociology and social science, as well as a justification of sociology and an account of how it should work. For Durkheim, the importance of sociology was to be found in its role in assigning value and increasing value in the institutions of modern society. As he explained,

> In fact, without doing violence to the meaning of the word, one may term an *institution* all the beliefs and modes of behaviour instituted by the collectivity; sociology can then be defined as the science of institutions, their genesis and their functioning. (Ibid., p. 45)

DOI: 10.1057/9781137577917.0004

This science of institutions and their functioning might appear as something as grand as Durkheim's work on religion and suicide. But Durkheim's role for the science of institutions is more mundane. By writing about 'functioning' Durkheim is repeating the instrumental argument about the value of social science. Sociology can help politicians make the right policies, and sociology can contribute to the economic well-being of the nation. As he put it later in the book, in a section that is also noted by his editor (Lukes, 1982, p. 21),

> There is no longer need to pursue desperately an end which recedes as we move forward; we need only to work steadily and persistently to maintain the normal state, to re-establish it if it is disturbed, and to rediscover the conditions, of normality if they happen to change. The duty of the statesman is no longer to propel societies violently towards an ideal which appears attractive to him. His role is rather that of the doctor: he forestalls the outbreak of sickness by maintaining good hygiene, or when it does break out, seeks to cure it. (Durkheim, 1982, p. 104)

The function of the government for Durkheim is to allow the nation-state to prosper economically, culturally and politically. Social science is useful, then, because it provides the rules of nation-states and their officials with the tools they need to ensure the continued prosperity of the nation. As Habermas (1989) shows, the ideals of modern government in this period are reduced to good management and the smooth running of bureaucracies and markets – just as they are today. Durkheim's vision of the value of sociology reduces social sciences to a form of 'hygiene' or 'cure' for the problems of social disorder, or a source of knowledge about normality. That very normality – rational bureaucracy, nationalism and capitalism – was and is politically contested, but the fact that social science turns those contested ideologies into the normal actually entrenches them even further in their hegemonic state.

Into the twentieth century, we can see this invisibility of such contested ideologies in much of the writing about the value of the social sciences. It becomes normal for socialists and liberals to agree that social sciences can help construct a better and more prosperous society, though they might differ in the role of the state and the role of the free market. Later on, social sciences are seen as commercially and politically valuable for the totalitarian states of Nazi Germany and the Soviet Union, as well as the new countries that emerge in the post-colonial era (Weindling, 1993; Wimmer and Glick Schiller, 2002). Social sciences are valued for their contribution to the 'effort' of progress, which becomes as ubiquitous in

DOI: 10.1057/9781137577917.0004

political speeches and newspaper columns then as GDP is today. Social science education and funding was then touted by politicians and social scientists as a necessity in the struggle for political supremacy in the world between Western empires (Wimmer and Glick Schiller, 2002). Social science knowledge was valued by writers across the political spectrum for its instrumental use, its economic and political impact. The Nazis used social sciences to re-shape their society and economy to one that excluded the Jews from the public sphere, as well as using social sciences to support their anti-semitism and their ultimate genocide (Weindling, 1993). It is often said that the Nazis were thoroughly modern and scientific in their planning and execution of the Holocaust (Arendt, 1973). But of course much of the planning was predicated on ideas about work and community taken from functionalist sociology, and modernist, rationalized management theory. In the prison notebooks of Gramsci, which were edited and published after his death (Gramsci, 1971), he sketches out a programme of educational reform that includes sociology and sociological epistemology and method as a core element. Gramsci's prison speculations show that members of the left believed in the normality of using the social sciences to improve planning and enable progress, political and economic theme. This theme can also be found in the non-fiction and diaries of George Orwell, who showed a strong belief in the importance of social science in changing society and helping society progress, through good governance (Orwell, 2009).

If it was only people outside social sciences, or on the fringes such as Gramsci, arguing for the instrumental value of social sciences, then we might think the argument tangential to what social sciences can actually provide. But social scientists themselves were central to the instrumental argument for their own work for much of the twentieth century. In the second half of the century, Talcott Parsons and functional sociology grew to dominate American sociology. Parsons and others in the Chicago School saw social sciences as having extrinsic value to governments and to the free-market system of modern capitalism (Parsons, 1964). In the United Kingdom, sociology became dominated by quantitative methods, and arguments for the usefulness of the social sciences to government (Kent, 1981), a debate that continues (Freese, 2007; Savage and Burrows, 2007). The Cold War saw social scientists playing a key role in finding ways to save the West from the threat of the Soviet Union, and the rise of big science, as we have seen, gave social science a financial and epistemological model to emulate (Fuller, 2000a). The social sciences,

DOI: 10.1057/9781137577917.0004

then, have always been enthralled by two related ideas – the idea that the social might be measured by a slide-rule or computer; and the idea that the social sciences might be a tool to make governments work efficiently and industries make bigger profits. It is time to look at some of the key social sciences in more detail: economics; psychology and sociology.

Arguments for economics from economists

How has economics made the case for itself? In its foundational stages, economics was presented as something completely rational and instrumental. Economics has always provided the tools for capitalism and for modern bureaucracies (Jones, 2014). It has underpinned the rise of the modern age, and the shift to globalization and post-modernity (Urry, 2007) by providing an epistemological justification for instrumentality. Adam Smith (1776) made the argument that humans make rational choices about the things they buy or sell, and the market operates through a universal law of supply and demand. That is, all action can be reduced to the instrumental question: what is the cost? If actions cannot be reduced to their value, they become unimportant or marginalized in economic models and policies. In the nineteenth and twentieth centuries, the science of economics became a matter of fact among the harbingers of modernity. If Smith and other classical economists were correct, free trade increased prosperity and fuelled societal progress. As we have already seen, governments across the West created laws and policies that nurtured the free market and the buying and selling of stocks and shares (Hobsbawm, 1988). This led to the enormous political success of Western nation-states and vindicated economists who argued for *laissez-faire* politics. But the success of the West could also be seen to be a vindication of economists who argued for planning and control by governments. Although Great Britain seemed to have become dominant through free trade, other nation-states followed economic theories that suggested such trade needed to be controlled, and that governments needed to take active measures to stimulate economic growth (Habermas, 1989; Hobsbawm, 1989). Whether the vindication was in favour of *laissez-faire* or various theories of intervention, the academic debates demonstrated the instrumental value of economics. This vindication allowed economists to become the new physicists, their theories couched in the language of mathematical science.

DOI: 10.1057/9781137577917.0004

Economists say we can therefore identify the laws of financial exchange and make predictions about the economy. We can measure the success of an economy through universally agreed measures such as the rate of inflation, or GDP, the aggregation of everything produced by each nation-state. In turn, say the economists, we can hold governments to account for their successes or failures against these measures (Jones, 2014). GDP, for example, has become seemingly the only way of measuring the success of a nation or a government. When GDP grows, the economy is judged to be okay, and the politicians are praised for their careful control of things. We are told that our economy is strong and booming, even though we might see empty shops, homeless people and workers struggling to pay their bills. All these things are not as important as the figure provided by the GDP model, which of course counts all the buying and selling in the financial sector as part of the national GDP. When the GDP shrinks everybody in the public sphere panics: governments are blamed and lose elections; bankers lose their jobs; and economists make money selling their ideas to magazines and television programmes. No one in the business news circus pauses to question the morality of GDP – is it right to continue to try to grow the economy in a world with finite resources, and massive environmental problems caused by the unrestrained competition between economies?

In the first half of the twentieth century, the dominant theory in economics was Keynesianism. Keynes believed that increased prosperity was a social good, because such wealth could be re-distributed to the poor through welfare, and through investment in work schemes and capital projects (Keynes, 1936). A good Keynesian government would be one that invested in social welfare, protected its industrial base through import tariffs, and which stimulated the economy through public spending at a time of recession. The American New Deal was a typically Keynesian intervention, driven by a combination of moral justice and instrumental need. In the years after the Second World War, Keynesianism contributed to the growth of liberal economics and free trade around the world, through the establishment of the United Nations, and then the European Economic Community and the trans-national financial institutions such as the World Trade Organization and the World Bank. These institutions resisted the idea that governments had to take full control of economics, as communism argued. Free trade had to be developed and nurtured as much as possible within a welfarist framework of government control (Helleiner, 1996). In Europe, Western countries and those in Scandinavia adopted social welfare policies as strong Keynesians.

DOI: 10.1057/9781137577917.0004

Since the 1950s laissez-faire has returned to dominate economic theory and the institutions that control the world economy. The Chicago School and its founder Milton Friedman have given the world the neo-liberal ideology that economies are held back by government spending and financial controls (Jones, 2014). Friedman's argument is that free trade has been proven to be the best way of organizing an economy in terms of sustained, long-term growth, so governments need to stop interfering in the mechanisms of the market (Friedman, 2009). The neo-liberals did not attract much support in political circles until the 1960s, when they started to intervene in the oppressive regime Indonesia (Klein, 2007). Then in the 1970s they found work in Pinochet's Chile, working for a dictator who followed their rules. They have a model of action for turning economies around and maintain them as healthy, progressive economies. They argue that struggling nations need to abandon constraints on free trade and movement of capital in and out of the country. They argue that governments have to sell their stakes in nationalized industries and privatize everything that can possible be privatized, from education to health, from the procurement of aircraft carriers to the cleaners in government buildings (Jones, 2014). Opening up economies to pure free trade is, they say, the only way to let the market work its magic to distribute wealth and resources in the most efficient way. Privatization should happen because it allows the magic of the free market to operate as widely as possible. Non-believers in neo-liberalism are mocked for their attachment to prejudices about welfare and old-fashioned ideas of government. Neo-liberal 'reform' is now the solution to any struggling country that has to go to the trans-national institutions for assistance (Klein, 2007).

Economics, then, is directly involved in the instrumental turn of social science, because it is directly involved in the justification of capitalism and the instrumentality of nation-states. It has created abstract models of the market and the economy that it insists are universal laws, and made a strong case for economists as the wise interpreters of those laws, because they are the only people trained in the maths and epistemological jargon needed to understand the work and its implications (Chang, 2011). Economics, then, apes the incomprehensibility and elite nature of theoretical physics. But theoretical physics at least is based on solid accounts of how the universe works and the limits of the laws of the material universe (Weinberg, 2015). Economic theory is more like the cabbala of medieval Judaism, a secret language of symbols signifying nothing but more mystery.

DOI: 10.1057/9781137577917.0004

Arguments for psychology from psychologists

Psychology's founders and popularizers have exhibited behavioural traits that may indicate some deep-rooted conflict over the value of psychology. Following the popular reception of *The Origin of Species*, Darwin set out to explore the biological origins of emotions in *The Expression of the Emotions in Man and Animals* (Darwin, 1872). Darwin was the first person to use modern science to understand and explain psychological problems. The idea that the tools of science could be used to unravel the philosophical problem of the minds – whether the mind was part of the body, or distinct from it, and it was distinct, what was it? – was appealing to the founders of psychology, such as William James (1890). The problem with the mind is that each of us knows we have one, or thinks so, and we know how our own minds interact with other people and the world. But we cannot know that other people have minds in the same way. Nor can we seemingly know where our mind is. Psychology, as the scientific study of the mind, offered a rational approach to exploring theories about the mind, and an experimental method that allowed a way of testing theories. Even if much of the methodological tools of psychology had yet to be developed, and so many of its claims were initially speculative, James believed this new science would be useful for the progress of human civilization. James saw psychology as a form of social science, which provided a different way to true knowledge than that offered by the natural sciences. As such, it could transform society by transforming knowledge about humans (ibid.). For some of the founders of psychology, then, it was firmly a social science that had a useful function in the modernization of society.

Others such as John Watson (1930) were convinced that psychology could be as scientific as biology, that is, he thought it could be assigned a place as useful and epistemologically correct as a natural science. The problem with psychology as it existed when Watson was writing was its speculative nature and its lack of methodological rigour. Watson believed much of what passed for theory was not only unproven, but it was unprovable. How can any experiment be undertaken to identify structures in the mind? Watson said they could not be found, so any theories that developed models of the internal workings of the mind had to be rejected. The only possible things that could be observed about the mind were behaviours, so psychology had to focus on the exploration of behaviours, the effects of internal workings out of sight. The exploration

DOI: 10.1057/9781137577917.0004

of behaviours then needed to be based on the scientific method: the controlled experiment. Such experiments could show how behaviours might be changed through external forces. This form of psychology was appealing to governments and corporations looking to modify people's behaviours: governments wanted more pliant and happy workers, and corporations wanted to make profits from selling products to consumers. At first though Watson's natural science form of psychology was not representative of the dominant psychological theories or schools. It was only later in the twentieth century that behaviourism was revived in the work of B. F. Skinner (1953) and others, where ideas of conditioning stimuli became adopted wholesale by advertising agencies, propaganda offices in nation-states and in the media (Packard, 1957).

One of the reasons for behaviourism's delayed rise to the mainstream in psychology was the dominance of psychoanalytical theories, such as those developed by Sigmund Freud (e.g., see Freud, 1997, 2003, 2005). Psychoanalysts believed that mental disorders in individuals could be traced to unconscious conflicts deeper in the minds of the sufferers. Freud believed that human minds developed through a number of stages in childhood, and normal adult minds were a synthesis of different structures in the mind, some conscious and some unconscious or subconscious. Mental disorders were caused by problems in this complex history and structure of the mind. A good psychoanalyst could use talking therapy or hypnosis to explore the ways in which the problems were manifested in images, beliefs, thoughts and dreams, and then the process of curing the problem would begin. These theories and practices were enormously popular in the first half of the twentieth century, and have continued to be engaged in by practitioners and patients. Freud and his peers offered the modern world an explanation for the increasing malaise felt by humans. We were all struggling with feelings we had for our parents; we were all traumatized by feelings of rejection as children; we were all driven by primitive urges to fight and have sex. These were the real reasons people felt dis-satisfied with modernity, with its popular culture and its commercialization – we were not offended by capitalism's hegemony and excess; we were playing out the Myth of Oedipus. Unfortunately for psychoanalysis, there was no evidence for much of the extravagant theoretical ontology, and no agreement on how and if any of it could be tested (Borch-Jacobsen and Shamdasani, 2012). But it proved immensely distracting to individuals in the modern age who were looking to validate their personal and professional life choices, and

DOI: 10.1057/9781137577917.0004

validated the individualization of consumerism, so it proved attractive at this time of fantasy futures and bourgeois lifestyles (ibid.). It has proven to be a continued source of theory for many in cultural studies, and runs through a large part of sociology, too (e.g., the work of Butler, 2006).

Perhaps as a result of the pseudoscientific nature of psychoanalysis, modern psychology has become even more scientific. Behaviourism is still an important feature of psychology, and underpins much of what is called applied social psychology. This is the practice of finding out what makes customers, employees, students or consumers make one choice rather than another. This is a lucrative part of psychology, and the findings are often turned into headline stories in the media, ahead of their adoption by interested parties such as corporations and institutions. The idea of nudging people to behave correctly, for example, is now part of the UK government's policies to tackle health problems and anti-social behaviour after being the subject of a bestselling book (Sunstein and Thaler, 2008; Vallgarda, 2012). The other important area of modern psychology with a value for corporations and governments is cognitive psychology. Unlike behaviourism, cognitive psychology does theorize structures of the mind, which are mapped onto parts of the brain. Manipulating the brain, then, opens up the possibility of improving the mind and behaviours associated with the mind, so governments are keen to consider the possibility that they might change citizens through such therapies.

Arguments for sociology from sociologists

I have discussed already many of the key defences of sociology made by the founders of the discipline and their successor through the twentieth century. But some more examples need to be highlighted to show the way on which instrumentality became a dominant form of rationality in sociology today. Sociology is the social science to which I align my own work, and in which much of the moral case for social sciences can begin to be made in its part in what I call 'critical sociology', as I will discuss in more detail in the next chapter.

Sociology has always had a strong critical element to its epistemological tradition, and through radical feminism and Marxism it has embraced the idea of theory as *praxis*, that is, doing sociology to reveal the mechanisms of oppression in late capitalism, and to provide space for political action against inequality and injustice. In the past

DOI: 10.1057/9781137577917.0004

sixty years, sociology has been the site of much heated debate about the extent to which this critical epistemology can be considered to be 'proper' sociology (Inglis, 2014; Potter, 2014; Savage and Burrows, 2007). For the proponents of the radical sociological approach, there is a key awareness of the ways in which higher education and the very idea of the scholar doing research are deeply problematic and contested parts of the structures of modernity. Radical sociologists have tried to challenge the norms of natural science, and the instrumentality of hegemonic power, because they see such things complement and justify one another (Fuller, 2000a). If science serves hegemonic power, then radical sociology tries to identify and disrupt that servile relationship. As I have discussed earlier in this book, this has led to many radical feminists turning towards rich, ethnographic, qualitative, naturalistic, ethical, person-centred research, designed to give voice to those on the margins while ensuring knowledge is co-produced with those who are being researched. This critical epistemology has been enriched by the post-modern or post-structural turn in cultural studies, which has led to a post-modern sociology interested in exploring the making of meaning and the fluidity of such meaning in a society that is post-modern, mobile, and global (Urry, 2007). Some of this post-modern sociology is deliberately provocative and playful in its concatenation of theory and popular culture; other parts of this post-modern sociology align with the radical sociological concern with making a space for political resistance to the hegemonic powers at work around us (Žižek, 2010).

Against this radical, then post-modern, sociology, much sociological research and theorizing has become deliberately positivist (Savage and Burrows, 2007). That is, many sociologists reject the idea that the natural sciences are a product of capitalism or hegemonic power, and believe that social sciences can use the methods of natural sciences to find out the truth about the social world. Although this positivist sociology does not have to be non-radical in its use of theory, and there are scholars who argue for a 'radical statistics' (see the activist academics and the journal at http://www.radstats.org.uk/), the majority of the work is limited to descriptive accounts of the social world, rather than explanatory accounts. The drive to do statistical research is backed by the learned societies of sociology around the word, which argue that such research is important because it provides generalizable findings, unlike the anecdotal, non-universal findings of qualitative research. So an ethnography of dark leisure among teenage boys is viewed as less important as a full

DOI: 10.1057/9781137577917.0004

survey of the relevant population, using a representative sample, because only the survey can tell us what 'really' happens. Many sociological departments in universities are dominated by scholars who specialize in various forms of quantitative analysis. Funding councils prefer research that uses the methodological tools of statistics, and journal editors favour such work because it has the 'stamp' of validity and rigour of the significance test. This kind of sociology is then a dominant kind across the global North, and especially in North America, where the Parsonian functional sociology continues to produce its findings undisturbed by the radial and post-modern turns that affected European sociology. In leisure studies, for example, there is a strong radical tradition in the United Kingdom, which favours qualitative research exposing issues such as the gender order and racism; but in North America, leisure studies, called leisure sciences, is still dominated by surveys exploring why people like to do certain things (Spracklen, 2009). And what is important about this on-going positivist sociological tradition is its value-claims: this positivist sociology says because it has access to the truth through its methods, and because it is unburdened by radical theory, it can be useful for the government and industry just like psychology and economics.

Regimes of instrumentality and governmentality in education and learning

The instrumental defence of social sciences makes the case that social sciences have some economic value, or some other impact on policy and governance. Everywhere in education and learning, we can find the same instrumentality at work. Going to university is no longer encouraged as something that develops young people as critical thinkers, or even as human beings, they are instead told that university will give them a better job (Docherty, 2015). In the United Kingdom, every university has senior managers devoted to employability and enterprise, demonstrating to students that courses lead to good jobs. Along with the focus on turning education and learning into skills development comes the new governmentality of key performance indicators, audits, league tables and performance development reviews, where the *panopticon* of modern power relationships keeps staff under constant surveillance (Foucault, 1973, 1980, 1991). Universities have to demonstrate to auditors and politicians that they are delivering employability

DOI: 10.1057/9781137577917.0004

through the number of students who get graduate jobs, or through the number of times students are given work placements. Lecturers have to show that they are finding income from consultancy as well as research, or making an impact through working with industry and/or policy-makers. Everything academics do is counted, even though the work of an academic – the long hours reading and marking, engagement with one's scholarly community, sitting around thinking – is impossible to reduce to a simple calculus. In this new regime of auditing and bureaucracy, the reality of what academics actually do is not important, instead we are audited on what the systems and the managers can understand. It is common practice across universities in the United Kingdom to assign and monitor every working hour to which we are contracted, so the monitoring takes no account of the hours we actually work. Managers routinely make decisions on the amount of teaching lecturers are given by deploying them up to the permitted maximum on their spreadsheets, with no sense that every individual and every course and module might have particular needs.

At the same time, academics are being measured by the impacts our research and scholarly activity might make. In the Research Excellence Framework and in applications to funding councils, as I have discussed, there is an in-built bias towards research that is of instrumental value because of its economic and policy impact. But the rhetoric of impact infects internal departmental meetings, academic boards and recruitment panels. Academic staff who bring in money through research and consultancy are celebrated by marketing managers and spin doctors, as well as the senior managers whose performance-related pay depends on such corporate game-playing. Human Resources managers create job descriptions and work criteria for academics that treat every lecturer, reader or professor exactly the same: the demands made on getting a job or being promoted into these posts are unrealistic on the social sciences and humanities, if taken seriously. To be a professor one has to demonstrate one is bringing in significant research funding, alongside making an impact and producing word-class outputs. These unrealistic job descriptions have come from management views about how natural sciences work, and a failure to understand that they cannot apply that beyond natural sciences (actually, it is probably unrealistic for many in the natural sciences, too, but it seems to be the normal practice). So far I have been lucky enough not to have my failure to 'win' funds and 'make a strong impact' count against me in my own university, but people

DOI: 10.1057/9781137577917.0004

around the world in this regime of instrumentality and governmentality are losing their jobs for failing to bring profit and honour to their universities (Docherty, 2015).

Regimes of global capitalism, hegemony and governmentality, then, have taken over universities, education and government planning. That much is clear. Everything we do is now measured, costed, and audited. Everything we do has to fit the instrumental narrative of universities being good for the economy, and places where students come to get a job afterwards. We might still think universities are sites of learning and research, but these are the symbols of an earlier age. In this age of instrumentality and governmentality, science is a tool of industry, and STEM subjects provide the epistemological and managerial models we all have to adopt. So the attempt to emulate STEM thinking in social sciences only serves to legitimize the instrumentality at the heart of this takeover. If social sciences make the case for their work and existence by measuring impact, measuring income-generation and fetishizing scientific methods, they allow themselves to be the subject of reduction to the 'big' natural sciences, and allow themselves to be subsumed.

DOI: 10.1057/9781137577917.0004

3
The Moral Case for the Social Sciences

Abstract: *Spracklen sets out three moral cases for the social sciences: they are good because they are rational inquiries; they are good because they help flourishing; and, most importantly, they are good because they show humans how to resist inequality. Spracklen makes the case that the ability to see the world through a critical lens is the necessary moral and social good that this critical sociology gives to the social sciences, and through the social sciences to the wider world. The social sciences are necessary and a moral and social good if humans are to live a freely communicative and moral life in a world dominated by hegemonic power, whether that power is built into belief systems, gender orders, popular culture, social classes or political constitutions.*

Spracklen, Karl. *Making the Moral Case for Social Sciences: Stemming the Tide.* Basingstoke: Palgrave Macmillan, 2016. DOI: 10.1057/9781137577917.0005.

DOI: 10.1057/9781137577917.0005

Finally, I come to the moral case for the social sciences. In this chapter I return to what I called critical sociology in the introduction, to make the case that the ability to see the world through a critical lens is the necessary moral and social good that this critical sociology gives to the social sciences, and through the social sciences to the wider world. I am making the case for a form of qualitative, critical, inter-disciplinary social sciences that draws on cultural studies, philosophy and political studies, as well as sociology. As I outlined in the introduction, I am using 'critical sociology' as a form of shorthand to define this critical, inter-disciplinary social sciences. The chapter begins with an exploration of the history of the idea of critical thinking as a means to acquiring knowledge about the good life, from Greek philosophy through belief systems and into the radial, secular Enlightenment values of the public sphere. In the second section I discuss sociological accounts of the importance of critical thinking, from Emile Durkheim through to others who have informed the inter-disciplinary lens of critical sociology, and my own understanding of it: C. Wright Mills, Michel Foucault, Stuart Hall and Jürgen Habermas. Then in the final section I discuss the importance of critical thinking in the world in which we live, which is a world of enormous inequalities of power. I will argue that the social sciences are necessary and a moral and social good if humans are to live a freely communicative and moral life in a world dominated by hegemonic power, whether that power is built into belief systems, gender orders, popular culture, social classes or political constitutions. I begin, then, by returning to the Greek philosophers.

The idea of critical thinking

> This is the display of the inquiry of Herodotus of Halicarnassus, so that things done by man not be forgotten in time, and that great and marvelous deeds, some displayed by the Hellenes, some by the barbarians, not lose their glory, including among others what was the cause of their waging war on each other. (Herodotus, 1920, 1.1.0)

As I discussed in the first chapter, the written ideas of the classical Greeks have survived as part of the Western epistemological tradition, and as its foundations. So they are necessary to understand the moral case for the social sciences, as their ideas permeate the way we think and the

DOI: 10.1057/9781137577917.0005

way we write about epistemology, ontology and ethics. When we turn to the Greeks, we can see the first clear defences of social sciences that have influenced our thinking, and which have survived to come down to us. In his book *The Histories*, Herodotus begins his account of the wars and political struggles between the Greeks and the Persians with a justification for his art. He has undertaken to inquire into the cause of the wars and to bring the story of the wars into one narrative, so that they will not be forgotten (Evans, 1991). He wants this work to be on display, that is, he wants it to be read and heard by people in public, so that people learn something true about the Persian wars, and something true about the Persians and other barbarians (Pritchett, 1993). What Herodotus is doing is constructing a systematic synthesis of different stories about the wars, and using his critical lens to make a rational assessment of the narratives most likely to be true (ibid.). He wants his readers to believe he has taken the time to master a range of data – other written accounts, material remains and conversations with respondents involved – to come up with a causal explanation, or a theory, of why the Persians and the Greeks were doomed to come to blows. Herodotus's history has, of course, been questioned for its lack of historical rigour, and its lack of credibility when it admits supernatural explanations into the story (Fehling, 1988) – but Herodotus is at least making an attempt to show that the tools of philosophy can be used to begin to make sense of the social and cultural spheres. Furthermore, Herodotus is not just writing history. In the book, he provides anthropologies of the Persians and other barbarians, showing his Greek audience the essential differences and similarities between them. This anthropological work may be weak and reliant in many cases on second-hand anecdotes and prejudices, but at least it shows that Herodotus is able to think critically about what counts as social evidence and social scientific explanation. It is in Herodotus that we see the argument first made that such inquiry was normal and justifiable for anyone learned in philosophy.

The Greek tradition of writing histories that used critical thinking to theorize causation and societal change continued into Roman and early Christian historiography, as I discussed briefly in the first chapter. These historians believed that it was possible to show their readers how things actually were and the reasons for their state of being. To be a critical historian, one needed to be able to make sense of the documents – the works of others and the primary sources – and to find out the relationships between the social, the cultural and the political. For

DOI: 10.1057/9781137577917.0005

early Christian historians, there was an added urgency to use critical historiographical skills to assess the authenticity of certain texts. This critical historiographical lens was adopted by Christian theologians and Muslim scholars, who each in turn needed to establish the veracity of truth-claims and anecdotes in various textual traditions (Russell, 2013).

Critical thinking in subjects we might call social sciences, such as sociology and political studies, was also an essential part of the Greek epistemological tradition. Greek philosophers did not distinguish between the natural and social, as I said in Chapter 1. But, furthermore, they positively saw the moral worth of social scientific thinking. That is, doing social sciences allowed them to make sense of the ethics of how societies are and may be constructed. In Plato's *Republic*, he reports a dialogue between Socrates and Glaucon about how cities and their societies have been and might be constructed. City-states at the time were generally organized around three kinds of government: oligarchy; democracy and tyranny. In *The Republic*, Socrates outlines these three as well as another, timocracy, as being forms of government that fall short of an ideal, utopian polity. Socrates argues that the ideal polity would be run by philosopher-kings, ones selected through a careful process and trained to be both wise and strong. Plato, through the words of Socrates, wants to argue that there is a moral and rational case for overhauling mainstream Greek society and making it more like that of Sparta:

'Very good. We are agreed then, Glaucon, that the state which is to achieve the height of good government must have community of wives and children and all education, and also that the pursuits of men and women must be the same in peace and war, and that the rulers or kings over them are to be those who have approved themselves the best in both war and philosophy.' 'We are agreed,' he said. 'And we further granted this, that when the rulers are established in office they shall conduct these soldiers and settle them in habitations such as we described, that have nothing private for anybody but are common for all, and in addition to such habitations we agreed, if you remember, what should be the nature of their possessions.' 'Why, yes, I remember,' he said, 'that we thought it right that none of them should have anything that ordinary men now possess, but that, being as it were athletes of war and guardians, they should receive from the others as pay for their guardianship each year their yearly sustenance, and devote their entire attention to the care of themselves and the state.' 'That is right,' I said. 'But now that we have finished this topic let us recall the point at which we entered on the digression that has brought us here, so that we may proceed on our way again by the same path.' 'That is easy,' he said; 'for at that time, almost exactly as now, on the supposition that

DOI: 10.1057/9781137577917.0005

you had finished the description of the city, you were going on to say that you assumed such a city.' (Plato, 1969, pp. 8.543a–8.543c)

This is a city that is assumed to be the best from the Socratic method – the application of logic to testing and rejecting or using every statement along the way – used to reach its ideal form and structure. Now at first, the ideal city-state dreamed of by Plato is obviously something instrumental in value. Plato wants to show his readers that his research project has a societal and policy impact. One can almost see the impact statement being written for the Hellenic Greek Research Excellence Framework, showing how Plato used his model to teach politicians how to write perfect constitutions. And this ideal city-state is not something we would want to live in, no matter the seductive idea that thinkers should be in charge of things. But the book is important because it shows us that Plato believes 'critical sociology', using the social sciences to think about the nature of society, is in fact a good thing, and an ethical thing. It is a good thing because Plato uses it without fear of ridicule – he is working in the tradition of every other Greek philosopher who ranged across all the sciences (Russell, 2013). And it is an ethical thing because it is part of the classical Greek tradition of using critical thinking to question power (Braund, 1994). The moral case for Plato's foray into the social sciences leads to an instrumental view of the city-state, but it is the moral case that starts off the inquiry – the fact there are no limits to what Plato (through Socrates) wants to theorize.

The moral case for social scientific inquiry is made more clearly and forcefully in the work of Aristotle. It is here that we hear the question: how do we live a good life? Aristotle wants his social sciences to be the tools of his political ethics (Aristotle, 1962). He wants to explore the different forms of society and culture to develop a reasoned model of human development, from which he then takes his ideal polity. But the moral case is more than just showing what constitutional forms or laws are the best for Greek city-states. Aristotle believes that what is ethical is associated with human activities that lead to increased *eudaimonia*, that is, happiness or well-being (Russell, 2013). This means that his ethics lead to practical conclusions. To understand how and why anything makes one happier, one needs to develop social scientific accounts of the mind, of culture and of society. *The Nicomachean Ethics* shows Aristotle developing a 'critical sociology', the way to establishing what exactly might lead us to that state of happiness (text in Bartlett and Collins, 2011). Establishing how much happiness, and what kind of happiness,

DOI: 10.1057/9781137577917.0005

is the best for humans to flourish is for Aristotle an empirical exploration combined with his knowledge of different states and histories. In Aristotle's mind, the best way to achieve *eudaimonia* is to live a virtuous life, where study is combined with leisure, and where pleasure is received in moderation (Fox, 2005). But his ethics give the social sciences a moral project. What he thought of as overall human flourishing is what we might and do think of as fairness. How do we create a social world in which all humans have the same sort of freedoms to develop and find happiness as humans? How can the Aristotelian goal of happiness be met by all of us? Answering this question is the purpose of the social sciences. We need the social sciences to reveal the inequalities and unfairness that get in the way of the Aristotelian ideal of well-being, and to show us ways in which we might have a more communicative, free and fair interaction with one another. This form of social scientific thinking and research continued to be central to the ethical philosophy of later Greeks such as the Stoics and the Epicureans (O'Keefe, 2009). Each of these schools of thought used social scientific thinking, critical sociology, to explore what they thought was the best way to live. They believed as well that such social scientific inquiry was legitimate, that it was possible to show there was a good way to live, because they wrote books and circulated their ideas widely (Morford, 2002).

In the Renaissance, the Greek idea that social sciences were a valid part of science that helped make sense of public and practical ethical problems was accepted by those radical humanists such as Erasmus who campaigned for political and epistemological freedoms (Lindberg, 2009; Russell, 2013). This belief in the moral surety of what I call critical sociology, thinking through an inter-disciplinary social science lens, became a feature of the Reformation and the wider humanist and philosophical trends of the early modern period. Thomas Hobbes's *Leviathan* is a classic political philosophy of this time, which uses thought experiments and critical thinking to build a model of human development and the power relations between citizens, sovereigns and states (Hobbes, 1996). In this work, Hobbes combines history with what we call sociology and psychology to argue that strong governments protect their citizens from the brutal and savage state of nature – that is, humans without laws will kill and be killed, so even though we become un-free when we form states with laws that constrain us, we willingly give up our freedoms for the security of those laws. Partly in response to the legitimation of absolutism in the work of Hobbes, John Locke constructed a theory of

DOI: 10.1057/9781137577917.0005

identity that argued we are each given the freedom to develop and think as free agents, and as such we all need to be given a measure of freedom to debate and choose the structures that govern us (Simmons, 1992). Locke also believed that religion and state should be separated, while religious differences needed to be tolerated, moves towards a secular state that allowed individual liberties to be protected (Habermas, 1989; Russell, 2013).

Locke's liberalism and psychological theories were influential on the later Enlightenment philosophers such as Voltaire, Hume and Kant. Each of these accepted the claim that the state had to be constructed in a way that allowed people to be free to debate and free to choose (Russell, 2013). The Enlightenment saw the construction of what Habermas (1989) identifies as the public sphere, a space between the privacy of domestic spaces and the functional spaces of government. The public sphere was a physical embodiment of the Lockean notion that humans need to be able to discuss and act freely with one another. In towns and cities across Europe people gathered in coffee houses, theatres and salons to gossip and be frivolous, and to discuss morally good matters such as culture, social and political reform and philosophy. The public sphere was the space where individual humans could be communicatively rational, using critical thinking to identify the moral and social problems with modern society. From this public sphere emerged thinkers such as Thomas Paine, who showed the logical fallacy of arguments defending privileges such as feudalism, monarchy and church (Paine, 1987). Paine was one of the many critical thinkers involved in the American Revolution, which resulted in the first attempt to write a political settlement on rational, critical, progressive grounds (even if the settlement excluded women and slaves), balancing freedoms with rights and responsibilities, promoting equality and democracy and ensuring hegemonic powers are themselves constrained. Paine was also present and involved in the French Revolution, which produced the Declaration of the Rights of Man and many radical measures inspired by critical sociological thinking. The first article and the sixteenth of the declaration state that

> Men are born and remain free and equal in rights. Social distinctions can be founded only on the common good.
>
> Any society in which the guarantee of rights is not assured, nor the separation of powers determined, has no Constitution. (https://en.wikipedia.org/

DOI: 10.1057/9781137577917.0005

wiki/Declaration_of_the_Rights_of_Man_and_of_the_Citizen, accessed 31 August 2015)

These articles show knowledge of sociology, psychology and political studies. The Enlightenment philosophers have already used their critical thinking to argue the veracity of the statements about equality, freedom and rights. In these articles are the moral case for critical sociology, and the moral case for the social sciences is also made. This is because they suggest that it is individual and collective responsibility to ensure that social distinctions are not made in an arbitrary or unjust manner. All citizens are equal, and their wealth and their family should not be measured. This is because we are all ultimately equal in the state of nature – all the wealth and power accumulated by others is given to them through unfair and hegemonic means. We might collectively decide to make someone a prime minister with powers to rule over us, but this is determined by the rules of the constitution we create and agree upon as equals. It is society, that is, the collective polity of every citizens, that is sovereign, not an arbitrary monarch or bishop.

Not all this social scientific debate led to radical, progressive political reform, however, and not all critical thinkers embraced what we might call a left-wing, radical politics. But even the reactionary authors of the Enlightenment era demonstrate the importance and normalcy of social scientific research and theorizing in their work. Edward Gibbon is one of my own personal heroes, even though his personal politics were reactionary (Burrow, 1985). His *History of the Decline and Fall of the Roman Empire* is a masterpiece of historiography that remains an important text for understanding the fall of the Roman Empire in the West and the successor politics in the West and in the East (Gibbon, 2005). It has enormous scope, but it is based on rigorous textual analysis. In the work, Gibbon blames the decline and fall of the Roman Empire on a number of long-term trends, but reserves his greatest contempt for the Empire's adoption of Christianity, which he argued weakened the manly virtues of Roman society: instead of leading armies, Romans became bishops and monks, and abandoned the defence of the borders to barbarian mercenaries. Although Gibbon's account of the social and cultural changes of the time are questioned by historians today (Burrow, 1985), his use of social scientific explanations in his historiography, and his appeal to the humanist and classical methods of analysis, show him to be part of the social scientific epistemology that emerged in the Enlightenment public sphere.

DOI: 10.1057/9781137577917.0005

The moral case for social sciences in critical sociology: from Durkheim to Habermas

Before I go on to make my own argument that there is a moral imperative to social science, I want to ground my argument in the moral case made by a number of influential theorists who range across what I call critical sociology. These are all people who have shaped this critical sociology in a positive way, people who have, in the language of impact management, 'world class' reputations in sociology, or cultural studies. They are all people who have shaped my own thinking about what is the point of doing this thing called critical sociology: Emile Durkheim, C. Wright Mills, Michel Foucault, Stuart Hall and Jürgen Habermas.

In the second chapter, I showed that Emile Durkheim was responsible for making the instrumental case for social science, arguing that sociology had an economic and policy impact and aligning his own work with many others who believed this was the key role for the social sciences, such as Herbert Spencer, Karl Marx and Max Weber (Alexander, 2014). But Durkheim did not only make this case – he believed that there was a moral case for social science, too. A good moral defence is to be found in *The Rules of Sociological Method*, where he writes:

> For what good is it to strive after a knowledge of reality if the knowledge we acquire cannot serve us in our lives? Can we reply that by revealing to us the causes of phenomena knowledge offers us the means of producing the causes at will, and thereby to achieve the ends our will pursues for reasons that go beyond science? But, from one point of view, every means is an end, for to set the means in motion it requires an act of the will, just as it does to achieve the end for which it prepares the way. There are always several paths leading to a given goal, and a choice must therefore be made between them. Now if science cannot assist us in choosing the best goal, how can it indicate the best path to follow to arrive at the goal? Why should it commend to us the swiftest path in preference to the most economical one, the most certain rather than the most simple one, or vice versa? If it cannot guide us in the determination of our highest ends, it is no less powerless to determine those secondary and subordinate ends we call means. (Durkheim, 1982, pp. 85–86)

Social science for Durkheim is important and necessary precisely because it does allow us to determine those highest ends. Social sciences are more than just epistemological methods that help determine means, the instrumental values of any given thing; for Durkheim, the value of social science is its ability to give us the tools and critical lens we need to

DOI: 10.1057/9781137577917.0005

articulate our ends – a fairer society – and a way to point out the ways in which such a society is hindered. Durkheim's claim that social sciences point out the route to these highest ends helps us realize that social sciences are political, and radical, because they are epistemologies of resistance, of challenge and of transformation. In sociology, this is clearly the foundation of the epistemological and ethical principles mapped out by C. Wright Mills in *The Sociological Imagination* (Mills, 2000). Mills wants his sociology to reveal what is hidden in plain sight, the structures that shape and constrain agency in modern society. He thinks everyone, not just academics, should be able to use their sociological imagination, by stepping out of any given situation and using the critical lens to ask: what is going on here?

Mills's sociological imagination is an aesthetically pleasing investigation, one which has to be done for its own ends – by making his sociology appeal to non-academics Mills wants everybody to enjoy the freedom of being critical and thinking sociologically. Doing the social sciences, for Mills, is good in itself, with no need for any other justification. This case for doing social science is moral because it appeals to the power of individuals to find interest in the social sciences *qua* social sciences. This egalitarian, internal justification for social sciences can be traced back to the communicative spaces of the public sphere (Habermas, 1984, 1989). But another and more important point for the moral case is Mills's vision that sociology is part of an emancipatory project designed to identify the hegemonies and power inequalities that have become normalized in late modernity (Gramsci, 1971). Using the sociological imagination for him becomes a political practice of talking truth to – or about – the power of elites. The sociological imagination is a useful entry point for students to critical sociology, making them realize how much of their 'normal' life, such as their leisure interests, are the product of social structures and struggles over the control of leisure and culture (Spracklen, 2009, 2013). It is not surprising to see his work still used in introductory courses on sociology, and referenced in sociology textbooks, because the idea is such a simple, yet powerful one. This is the whole purpose of the social sciences: to see the social world as it actually is and to help constrained and marginalized agents effect change where they can (Lynd, 2015).

Michel Foucault is important to critical sociology because his work is truly inter-disciplinary, ranging from history and philosophy through sociology and cultural studies and radical politically (Foucault, 1972, 1973, 1980, 1991, 2006). As a historian of science Foucault shows us how what

DOI: 10.1057/9781137577917.0005

is considered to be a science is always the result of political struggles for power (1972, 1980, 1991, 2006). The things we believe to be true or false, or right and wrong, are also subject to the rise and fall of particular epistemological traditions (Foucault, 1973). One might think that Foucault is not the person to turn to when trying to make a moral case for the social sciences, as his work seemingly critiques the notion that there is a morality independent of social and political discourse (Foucault, 2006). But Foucault's work makes that moral case through its example. If Foucault is rightly suspicious of any discussion of morality and ethics and truth, he writes extensively about the ways in which capitalism and its allies in the sciences work to control and marginalize the working classes and others (Foucault, 1980, 1991). He uses critical sociology to reveal the way commodification and postmodernity have brought us a new order of embodiment, where our place in the social structures is written physically onto us in material products (Foucault, 1991). He uses critical sociology to reveal the ways in which sexuality has been shaped and controlled by those in power in any given society (Foucault, 2006). Foucault, then, is on the right side of the argument, that is, he is on the radical, progressive side that sees social sciences as a way of revealing the truths of power, just like Durkheim and Mills. He may have critiqued Marxists for failing to recognize the historical transformations that he thought were changing modern society, but Foucault still aligns himself with the left (Foucault, 1980). Doing the work of social sciences, the work of critical sociology is fundamentally important to his epistemological project and his radical politics.

Although he was and is juxtaposed with Foucault in many textbooks and student essays, Stuart Hall shares with Foucault a common commitment to radical politics and the emancipatory potential of critical sociology. Hall has done more than anyone else to popularize the theories of Gramsci (1971), and in particular the idea that power in capitalist structures is hegemonic when the capital class has full control of the media and culture (Hall, 1993, 1995, 1996, 1997, 2002, 2011). Hall's work cuts across sociology, cultural studies, history, philosophy and political studies, but has a common purpose: to show the ways in which marginalized, subaltern groups and individuals are constructed as deviant outsiders by the ruling, hegemonic class of late-modern society. Hall comes from the radical, post-Marxist turn to community, culture, class and 'race' in the 1970s, starting his contribution to critical sociology by being one of the editors of the classic text *Resistance through Rituals* (Hall and Jefferson, 1976). In

DOI: 10.1057/9781137577917.0005

this text, Hall and his contributing colleagues show how young people use sub-cultural spaces and fashions to define identity and belonging against the tide of regulations and restrictions placed on them by governments, police and the mainstream media. In one of his recently published essays, Hall (2011) analyses the rise of neo-liberal ideology, its historical origins and its normalization in the post-industrial and post-colonial West. He ends by wondering if its dominance has become total:

> Is neo-liberalism hegemonic? Hegemony is a tricky concept and provokes muddled thinking. No project achieves a position of permanent 'hegemony'. It is a process, not a state of being. No victories are final. Hegemony has constantly to be 'worked on', maintained, renewed and revised. Excluded social forces, whose consent has not been won, whose interests have not been taken into account, form the basis of counter movements, resistance, alternative strategies and visions... and the struggle over a hegemonic system starts anew. They constitute what Raymond Williams called 'the emergent' – and the reason why history is never closed but maintains an open horizon towards the future... In ambition, depth, degree of break with the past, variety of sites being colonized, impact on common sense and everyday behaviour, restructuring of the social architecture, neo-liberalism does constitute a hegemonic project. Today, popular thinking and the systems of calculation in daily life offer very little friction to the passage of its ideas. Delivery may be more difficult: new and old contradictions still haunt the edifice, in the very process of its re-construction. (Ibid., pp. 727–728)

Hall's critical sociology reveals the truth about the ideology that has shaped the power relationships in contemporary society. This is the moral case for his work. Hall then sees critical sociology as a way of identifying those contradictions, the logical inconsistencies and the ruptures that Gramsci (1971) says necessarily leave any hegemonic project incomplete. His citation of Raymond Williams (1977, 1981) points to another moral case for the social sciences. Our task is to explore, reveal and nurture the emergent counter-hegemonic forces and cultures that Williams argues will inevitably appear at a time of hegemonic culture.

The final contribution to the moral case for the social sciences comes from Jürgen Habermas (1984, 1987, 1989, 1998, 2000, 2008). In the work of Habermas, we see the ideal of the critical sociologist, interlacing historical and philosophical arguments to make public interventions about the moral importance of sociology (Habermas, 2000, 2008). His theoretical project shows how the public sphere was constructed at the time of the Enlightenment through what he calls communicative

DOI: 10.1057/9781137577917.0005

rationality (Habermas, 1984, 1989). Communicative rationality is the free discourse and dialogue between equals, modelled on the methods and ethics of scientific debate but which informs all liberal and radical politics. This rationality, for Habermas, is a fundamental part of being human, and in the public sphere it is given its fullest space to construct modern society and culture. But Habermas (1987), following Weber (1992), says that late-modernity changes the dominant rationality to that of instrumentality. This happens when the model of capitalism, the model of the nation-state and the model of natural science converge, which enables thinking beyond its economic value, or its function in the management systems of the workplace and the government. In this era of instrumentality, culture and leisure have become commodified, as argued by Adorno (1991) and Habermas (1987). Education has become part of the system of instrumentality (Habermas, 1984, 1987). But universities and by inference the social sciences remain for Habermas spaces where the lifeworld of humanity, the remnant of the public sphere of the Enlightenment, can be found (Spracklen, 2009). For Habermas, the social sciences can and should be used to protect this lifeworld and communicative rationality and action, and social scientists should engage in meaningful, critical dialogue with those outside universities who want to act to challenge instrumentality in its own realm (e.g., on leisure, see Spracklen, 2009).

Making the moral case for social sciences

There are three moral cases for the social sciences, all of which emerge from the claims and arguments made by writers both ancient and modern. All three are inter-connected and depend in part on one another. My moral case for the social sciences will therefore use the three cases from these earlier defenders of the social sciences, but I will show that it is the third moral case that is the most important today. The three moral case for the social sciences are as follows: first of all, the study of social sciences is a thing in itself that is worthy of study for the pleasure of doing and finding things out; second, the study of social sciences allows us to flourish as humans and develop as happier and equal individuals; and third, the study of social sciences allows us to resist the instrumentality, injustice and inequality that make up the norms and values of our late-modern society.

DOI: 10.1057/9781137577917.0005

A thing in itself with its own justification

We owe it to the Greeks that the pursuit of knowledge and engaging in what they loosely defined as 'science' or philosophy is considered a legitimate practice for a human. Classicist values have then shaped the epistemological tradition and pedagogical systems we have inherited in the modern world. There is a default moral defence of all sciences and arts as being part of the common culture of humanity, and things that are the common inheritance of humanity (Docherty, 2015). The social sciences are one part of this epistemology and method of knowing and finding things out, and no one part of that is more important than another. When modern universities were first developed as teaching institutions controlled by researchers and scholars, they were envisaged as spaces for the protection and creation of this scientific material and epistemological culture (Lightman, 1997). Degree courses and individual schools and departments might have specialized around disciplines; each university was supposed to nurture all disciplines and subjects equally. Social sciences were developed in this moral enterprise as disciplines falling within the sciences more broadly, but sharing ideas and objects with the arts. The social sciences, then, are important and necessary because they are part of the wider moral purpose for education and rational inquiry. Education allows us to transmit the sum total of human knowledge to the next generation, so it is necessary to include the social sciences as they are part of the sum total of human knowledge.

Rational inquiry is the pursuit of new knowledge, which should be allowed to be free from interference or constraint. There is a belief that doing this activity is worthy in itself, justifiable to no one but the individual undertaking the inquiry. The pursuit of knowledge *qua* knowledge is its own end, and knowledge production should be left un-fettered because that is how we come to knowledge. In the natural sciences, there are strong defences of this kind of inquiry: theoretical physicists and pure mathematicians argue that they need to be allowed to think unconditionally about the things they think are important to them, because that is how their fields advance. The idea that any knowledge production has been free from constrain in the past is of course problematic, as I have shown in this book: all knowledge production is controlled. But there is a belief in the Western epistemological tradition, taken from the Greeks, perfected in the public sphere, that the pursuit of knowledge should be free, that is, it should not be subject to account to rulers or managers. In some universities, senior managers and leaders take the moral case

DOI: 10.1057/9781137577917.0005

for academic freedom so seriously that they make sure their portfolio of courses covers everything: from arts and humanities, through the social sciences, to the natural sciences and engineering. These same decision makers foster a university culture where diversity of opinion and inquiry among academic staff is valued. But in the vast majority of universities, the ideal of a universal space for learning and finding things out is under threat. There is pressure every day on scholars to justify their instrumental worth, and the claim that we should be allowed to research anything and everything that interests us for its own sake is seen as old-fashioned, or naïve. The danger of STEM thinking becoming dominant in the social sciences is that it immediately over-turns this moral case, and immediately makes social sciences seem less important than natural sciences.

Despite the historical specificity of the universal body of knowledge, and the rational inquirer doing their own thing, the general point is still a necessary one. We must not lose the knowledge that we have constructed as rational inquirers, and we must not let the instrumentality of today weaken the continued engagement in the pursuit of knowledge for the sake of knowledge. And we must defend all the forms of knowledge and rational inquiry that have ended up within the universities and the idea of critical thinking and inquiry (even if we admit that there are some kinds of knowledge – mystical, irrational – that are not part of the secular university). So we must accept the social sciences as part of that tradition, practice and future. That means, of course, that we accept natural sciences and the arts and humanities, whether we as social scientists think poorly of them. Doing this study for the study is worthy and necessary. So it is true that the social sciences are worthy of study as things in themselves. Education and rational inquiry are moral goods, which should be protected and nurtured for their own sakes. If we do not accept that, we give up on the idea of common humanity, on the idea of progress and on the idea that we can construct knowledge that takes us away from the arbitrary and the irrational.

A thing that allows us to flourish as humans and develop as happier and equal individuals

Social sciences are well-placed to contribute to Aristotle's ethical programme of *eudaimonia*. If the moral purpose of rational inquiry is to allow us to flourish as humans, then the social sciences are the key to achieving this end. We cannot flourish as humans without a deep and meaningful social science critical lens. Only through an understanding of the social world and the relationships between humans can we begin to flourish as humans. The Greeks acknowledged this important role for what we call social sciences. For them, as I have shown earlier in this book, there was no difference between thinking about the movement of stars and the types of polity that existed. Thinking about social relations, about culture and about political structures enabled them to develop ethical positions on the good life, whether it was best to intervene in the wider world to introduce improved constitutions and models of governance, or whether to withdraw from political action to foster the good life through individual study and leisure (Fox, 2005). How to flourish as humans, how to live a good life, is the foundation of the Western epistemological tradition, and as Bertrand Russell (2013) shows, much of what passed as philosophy from the time of Marcus Aurelius through to the Enlightenment was actually what we might call social ethics: the application of social scientific thinking – about our inner selves, about our relationships with others, about the structures that bind us and the materials we create – to solving the question of how to live good. Most of this social ethics used thought experiments rather than doing what we would call research, so it was limited, but it did create the space intellectually for the research and rational inquiry around the good life that founded the social sciences.

With the growth of the social sciences as legitimate academic disciplines, this search for the moral centre of the good life, the end of human flourishing, continues to play a significant but often overlooked part of each social science discipline's foundations and assumptions. Individuals turn to the social sciences to find out how we can possibly lead a good life that gives us a sense of fulfilment (Potter, 2014). The social sciences, in return, offer a space and ways of thinking that show what things might be part of that human flourishing. The social sciences should be the sciences that allow us to fully grasp the scope of human flourishing, because only the social sciences concerned themselves with humans, cultures and the social world. So, for example, social sciences such as psychology are at the forefront of the pursuit of happiness. Is happiness as important to human flourishing as Aristotle claimed, and if it is, how do we become happier as individuals? Is it possible to find some way of living that makes us happier and more contented? Psychology allows us to weigh up different theories or models of happiness and explore how different social and cultural spaces and practices might impact on our happiness. Sociology allows us to develop a broader theory of happiness within modern society, and the forms of work, leisure and culture that might make us more or less happy. In human flourishing, we might think that health and well-being are important, and the social sciences again are crucial to establishing the social and cultural bases of ill-health, and the ways in which certain spaces and activities might improve health and well-being (Bastow, Dunleavy and Tinkler, 2014). This work might be used by policy-makers, because they want healthier consumers and voters, but that instrumental appropriation of the social scientific contribution to human flourishing does not alter the fact that the rational inquiry begins with the moral case of helping humans flourish and live good lives.

The social sciences show us that human flourishing works best when humans have equal access to material and cultural goods. This may have been assumed by liberals and radicals in the age of the Enlightenment and beyond, but the social sciences have made the case for the utilitarian value of equality: that equality and freedom create the best conditions for the maximum amount of happiness and good for the greatest number of people (Russell, 2013). The social sciences provide the tools and knowledge to promote greater equality and freedom, and the moral justification for challenging inequality (Hall, 2011; Habermas, 1998, 2000). Human flourishing depends on each of us being able to think and act communicatively with one another. The social world should be a Habermasian lifeworld, where people interact freely to develop as humans, to learn and to discuss and to create new forms of culture and social life (Habermas, 1984, 1987). Leisure, for example, becomes a space and an activity that is valued because it is entered into freely as a means to communicate with others, set against the constraints of work and family (Spracklen, 2009, 2011). But the value of leisure can be and often is ruined by the transformation of leisure into an industry of consumers and providers. The social sciences can say that this is what the social world should be if all humans are to actualize their potential as humans, even if in reality the social world is constructed in a way that marginalizes certain social groups, and in a way that favours and gives power to the elites (Gramsci, 1971; Hall, 1993; Williams, 1981). The social sciences, then, allow us to flourish as humans because they show us how to live the good life, and show us how to construct and defend the communicative lifeworld in which such flourishing happens. The social sciences show that the good life is a free and equal life and make the moral case that human flourishing works

DOI: 10.1057/9781137577917.0005

when we are given the freedom to find our identity, our self, our place in the world. The social sciences are a force for social and moral good. They show each of us that there is a better world, a better way to live, which will allow us to actualize and humans, to protect the lifeworld and to be happier. If this was the end of my moral case, this would be enough, I think, to convince readers of the importance of social sciences as social and moral good. But the example of critical sociology can take this even further, to the third and final moral case for social sciences.

A thing that allows us to resist the instrumentality, injustice and inequality that make up the norms and values of our late-modern society

Critical sociology is at the heart of my moral argument for the social sciences. Critical sociology tells us that the world is filled with hidden forces that shape the social, cultural and political spaces through which we move. These hidden forces are the forces that have constructed our late-modern or post-modern society. In the global North, the earlier imperialist hegemonies of the West still retain a cultural power and political hegemonic grip on global society. We still live in a world where capitalism creates enormous inequalities, with a global elite moving freely from city to city, while the lower classes drown in their thousands illegally crossing the seas in search of security and freedom. We live in a world where neo-liberalism has seemingly triumphed, where bankers are rewarded for their lack of morals but politicians who try to resist the neo-liberal, austerity ideology, such as the 2015 Syriza government in Greece, are ridiculed or forced to compromise (for the prelude to the affair, see Stavrakakis and Katsambekis, 2014). We live in a world where national-ism still shapes and controls the daily lives of citizens, through actual wars to the proxy wars of professional sports, while national democracy and autonomy is arrogated to unelected bankers and policy-makers in trans-national organizations and corporations. We live in a world where money and the control of it dictates which humans flourish and which ones struggle. This world is one where the gender order still operates to normalize social and cultural differences as natural differences, where it is nearly always assumed to be right for men to hold positions of power, where women are treated as inferior in most cultures and belief systems. This is a world where white, Western people and nation-states took power through military and economic superiority, and where hierarchies of race

DOI: 10.1057/9781137577917.0005

make minority ethnic groups in nation-states, whether indigenous or long-standing, or recent migrants are treated as dangerous subalterns – as criminal Others who pose a threat to national security and national identity. This is a world where trans-national corporations and the elites conspire to control land and resources in their own interests, creating crises of affordable land and housing, while at the same time destroying the world though pollution and environmental catastrophes: as humans starve in refugee camps, animals become extinct and new oil wells are drilled. This is a world where the instrumental logic of the economic bottom line leads to the end of all resources, and the end of any economic growth with the end of modern civilization. We live in a world where these obscene social inequalities lead to the rich minority living longer, where their children get better education and better cultural capital, where the hegemons pass on all their power and privilege as if the political revolutions that ended feudalism never happened. All this happens as the elites keep control of the media, giving people the stories they want people to hear, scaring voters and citizens into allowing security agencies to take their liberties away (Hall, 2011).

I make no apology for this negative state-of-the-world address. Everything wrong about the world today is a consequence of the system that has shaped our society. In short, the society in which we live is the society of modernity, the society of capitalism and the society of hegemony. The people who have power in our society do not want to give that up. They want to retain the system that had brought them enormous power and wealth because they have been given that enormous power and wealth. The inequalities that exist within the neo-liberal, late-modern society may well cause some of these elites sleepless nights, and some of the more moral of the elites might feel bad enough to invest their wealth and power on philanthropic endeavours (Dawson, 2013). Some apologists for neo-liberalism will inevitably argue that the excess profits of capitalism trickle down to the rest of society, through increased prosperity for all, or increased choices for all (Friedman, 2009). But as Marx has told us, the inequalities and injustices in the system need to be there for the system to generate the wealth and power for the elites (Marx, 1992). That is, the system's instrumentality works to make the inequalities become greater.

This is where we need to return to critical sociology, and from there to social science more broadly. It is in critical sociology that we find the methods and theoretical frameworks to make sense of this modern state of society. To understand what is happening, what is morally wrong, we need critical sociology's radical politics. We need to align the social sciences with the politics of critical sociology. Critical sociology allows us to abandon the notion of objectivity for a more subjective rational inquiry: we need to align ourselves with the majority of humanity that is marginalized by inequality, and against the minority who are taking an unjust share of power, wealth and resources. And critical sociology does not just show us what is wrong with the world. It allows us to see a way to resist the wrongs, to make a counter-hegemonic challenge. Critical sociology, as I will discuss in the conclusion, offers ways to recover the good life and ways to overturn the gross inequalities imposed by the system of instrumentality. The moral case for social sciences is that critical social sciences, of any variety, allow us to make sense of the hegemony that has made the world the way it is. The critical forms of the social sciences force us to stand up to fight for what is morally correct: equality and freedom. The social sciences are necessary and a moral and social good if humans are to live a freely communicative and moral life in a world dominated by hegemonic power, whether that power is built into belief systems, gender orders, popular culture, social classes or political constitutions.

DOI: 10.1057/9781137577917.0005

Conclusion

Abstract: *Spracklen concludes by repeating the argument that critical sociology, critical thinking across the social sciences, is morally necessary because it reveals the truth about the abuses of power that hold the majority of the world's population in positions of marginality. This final moral case is the Marxist one, or the radical feminist one, or the one from Critical Race Theory: we need critical thinking to reveal the truth about the gross inequalities that are a product of modernity, instrumentality and global capitalism. Spracklen appeals to all social scientists to embrace this call and this moral case, and to work to ensure the moral case is central to their teaching and their research, then suggests practical steps that might be taken to help social scientists resist the pressure to be instrumental in their work.*

Spracklen, Karl. *Making the Moral Case for Social Sciences: Stemming the Tide.* Basingstoke: Palgrave Macmillan, 2016. DOI: 10.1057/9781137577917.0006.

Although I have enormous sympathies with the politics of the nine-teenth-century social movement, I am not a luddite, one of those radical campaigners fighting the factory system. I do not want to rip up the machinery of modernity, and I do not want to turn the clock back to a pre-modern, agrarian society. I know the modern world is better in many ways than the pre-modern. I know the importance of the incredible advances made in science, technology, engineering and medicine. This morning, for instance, I caught an electric train to work. Without this technological advance it would be impossible for me to live in the town where I live and work in the city of Leeds, because the distance separating them is thirty miles. I am a commuter, a middle-class product of the modern age, given an education and well-paid job in higher education that allows me to live far more comfortably than any of the housemaids, factory workers, brick-layers, housewives, caretakers and miners from whom I owe my genes. I sit here in my office listening to recorded music on my computer, typing on word-processing software. There is no need for me to write anything by hand anymore. But science and technology are not just about transport and silicon chips. The advances in medicine and public health surround me and make me and my loved ones healthier than we would have been before the rise of STEM in the age of modernity. My father would have been crippled, suffering in agony, if it was not for the pills he takes that combat his arthritis. My own life would have been very short if it wasn't for the doctors and nurses, and the equipment in the hospital, which ensured I stayed alive when I stupidly crawled out of a high window as a toddler.

The rise of STEM, then, has brought obvious advantages to many of us. STEM works by giving us a method that allows us to find out the truth about the world, so that we can solve problems, such as building electric trains and developing drugs that ameliorate the symptoms of arthritis. The problem is, the truth is valuable to those with the economic and cultural capital to exploit it. STEM was and is part of the instrumental-ity of capitalism. Reducing problems to their undying truth makes one susceptible to a category error of accepting the reduction of STEM to its economic value. In turn, the confidence of STEM makes STEM knowledge attractive to capitalists and the hegemons of empires and nation-states. Knowing how to make trains gives one an economic advantage over one's rival, whether one is a corporation or a nation-state. Owning the rights to such knowledge products becomes an important part of modern capital-ism and leads to the development of the Big Science of the second half of

DOI: 10.1057/9781137577917.0006

the twentieth century, where most research in STEM becomes dominated by hegemonic interests, whether the military building new weapons or trans-national corporations buying up patents for chemicals that may cure diseases (Fuller, 2000a, 2000b; Goldacre, 2008).

As I have shown in this book, the dominance of STEM today is a product of its instrumental value to hegemony, as much as it is to its epistemological value, which anyway is inextricably inter-laced with the instrumental value. This means that all sciences, natural and social, as well as every other form or rational inquiry situated in a university, are judged by the reductive logic of STEM. This leads to the imposition of neo-liberal management structures on academics, as STEM thinking leads to the acceptance that it is normal for all of us to show our impact in the wider world. For research groups in biochemistry it is easy to show that their research can lead to some drug or food product that will create patents and profits, so it is easy for them to bid for and find funding from research councils and corporations. When research groups in sociology are compared to these high-impact, high-funding groups, they cannot compete, and are often demeaned by senior managers and critics in the public sphere. The response in the social sciences to this rise of STEM thinking in the public sphere has been to copy the language. The Campaign for Social Science tries to defend the social sciences through showing that social sciences are just like the natural sciences – we can do proper science; we can do statistics and experiments; and we can make money and help governments do their work more efficiently. I can sympathize with the moral dilemma of such campaigns. I am sure the good people at the Campaign don't just want to make the instrumental case, and I am sure they would agree with most of what I have said about the moral importance for social sciences, and the danger of the instrumental case. They are having to make the case in such a way because we live in a world where profit and policy impact are the only two measures policy-makers, chief executives and politicians really understand. Then Campaign needs to keep those people on-side, as it were, because the consequences would be huge reductions in funding for the social sciences, and complete isolation from the decision-making centre.

But if the campaigners for the social sciences at these high levels are reluctant to make the moral case, it is up to the rest of us to make that case. I have shown in the last chapter there are three moral cases to make to defend the social sciences: first of all, the study of social sciences is a thing-in-itself that is worthy of study for the pleasure of doing, and

DOI: 10.1057/9781137577917.0006

finding things out; second, the study of social sciences allows us to flourish as humans and develop as happier and equal individuals; and third, the study of social sciences allows us to resist the instrumentality, injustice and inequality that make up the norms and values of our late modern society. The first moral case is based on the idea of learning for learning's sake, the value at the heart of the modern university, and much of modern education. The social sciences are valuable because they are one part of the portfolio of subjects we critically and rationally explore and study as modern humans. The second moral case is based on the Aristotelian idea that the sciences, loosely defined, are good because they help humans to flourish. The social sciences are ideally placed to meet this end as they are the source of much of the thinking and evidence around the morality and ethics of the good life. The third moral case is the most important one, and is founded on the critical sociology I defined in the introduction. Critical sociology, critical thinking across the social sciences, is morally necessary because it reveals the truth about the abuses of power that hold the majority of the world's population in positions of marginality. My final moral case is the Marxist one, or the radical feminist one, or the one from Critical Race Theory: we need critical thinking to reveal the truth about the gross inequalities that are a product of modernity, instrumentality and global capitalism. I appeal to all social scientists to embrace this call and this moral case, and to work to ensure the moral case is central to their teaching and their research.

I am aware this may sound incredibly naïve of me. The remainder of this conclusion will look at the challenge we might have to ensure this notion of critical thinking and morality is not dismissed as utopian, idealistic or old-fashioned by the decision makers in education and the Academy. I will then suggest practical steps that might be taken to help social scientists resist the pressure to be instrumental in their work.

Making the moral case for social sciences: in practice

What do we do as critical social scientists? The first thing we need to do is to identify others like us in the system. That means finding critical social scientists in our own networks and our own places of work. This should be relatively straightforward for those aligned with sociology, maybe less straightforward for those aligned to other social sciences. We need to build formal and informal groups and network of radial or

DOI: 10.1057/9781137577917.0006

critical social scientists. In our places of work, we need to speak to one another as equals, support each other against the neo-liberal managerial regimes of power and build strategic alliances across departments and schools. We then need to gain control over the curriculum across the social sciences. This might be a hard task but we have every right to say what we think should be in the curriculum for undergraduates and post-graduates. If we allow courses and modules to be designed and approved by colleagues who think instrumentally, we fail to provide our students with the critical thinking that will help them see through the inequalities of the world. It is our moral duty to ensure there is a critical element to all the social sciences we teach. If we are in charge of a module (what North Americans might call a course), we need to lobby the degree course leader to change and update the content to make it more critical. If we are in charge of a degree course (what North Americans might call a programme) we need to make sure the content is strongly critical, and is being delivered by teachers who understand the need to be critical. For postgraduate research programmes, we need collective action within each university to ensure the social sciences are not marginalized by the natural sciences; but we also need to defend critical social sciences as being important and necessary, without compromising with the STEM discourse and STEM thinking.

In our own networks, we need to build organized groups of critical social scientists. This might mean getting involved with organizing and planning inter-disciplinary conferences and workshops. It might mean creating our own journals, writing our own monographs and working on collaborative research programmes. Or it might mean setting up or join-ing and running special interest groups within the social science learned societies. Ultimately, we need to establish people like us in positions of responsibility within these learned societies. The politics of learned soci-eties might feel remote and boring for many academics, filled seemingly as it is with discussions about membership fees and prizes, but learned societies are a vital part of our community: they represent our commu-nity in the eyes of the outside world. So we need to actively involve ourselves in them. That is, we need to make sure these learned societies promote the moral purpose of the social sciences, even if they are forced to make the instrumental case to partners in corridors of power.

Beyond our networks, we need to create alliances with radical social movements and other citizen's groups aligning themselves to the left within the public sphere. We need to support political parties standing

DOI: 10.1057/9781137577917.0006

against the tide of global capitalism and for progressive causes. We need to add our voices to the organizations fighting the destruction of the environment, or the privatization of culture and space, or the enormous increase in surveillance and control, all issues that have pressing urgency. We have the knowledge and the critical thinking tools to help these activists, and we need to join with them in their protests and actions where we can make a difference. In the sociology of leisure, for example, much good work has been done by activist-academics working with football supporters resisting the takeover of their clubs, or resisting the xenophobia and racism that is normalized within football (Brown, 2008; Millward, 2011). This is our version of impact – not what we can do to turn a profit or make better government, but how we can combat capitalism, and its instrumentality and hegemony in everyday lives. If we can get our ideas into the wider sphere relatively unmediated, that is good, but we need to beware of press offices and news desks seeking stories and lines to fill space, because that is when our research and our arguments might be distorted, or mocked. Where we are careful, we might want to extend our engagement with the outside world by talking directly with people who work for governments and corporations, but this has to be on our own terms, and without any promises of returns or value. We need to be careful about chasing research and consultancy funding. It is morally correct to seek funding from a research council to do research we may have done anyway, but it is morally wrong to take money from corporations or governments to solve a problem for them. That said, we need to use our collective strength, through the learned societies and our activist networks, to persuade governments and policy-makers in education to place the social sciences and its critical lens in the core of the curriculum in schools.

Scholars within each subject or discipline within the social sciences will need to work out for themselves how best to take on the challenge of putting the moral at the core of their work. I am not going to try to cover all the social sciences, but I do need to say something about three of the biggest ones: sociology, psychology and economics.

For sociology, there is a need not to be complacent about the centrality of what I have called critical sociology to this moral case. A large part of sociology remains un-critical, in thrall to simple functionalist theories of human interaction, or dependent on copying the methods of natural sciences. While there is a space for both of these kids of sociology, the mainstream of sociology needs to be the critical kind. Further, sociology

DOI: 10.1057/9781137577917.0006

needs to return to the critical and structural, and get beyond the post-structural hiatus that has left it lacking in confidence in its own veracity. There is much that is important in post-structuralism, but it has left sociology tied up in debates about the certainty of truth, precisely when we need to say that there is a truth about the use and abuse of power in the modern world.

For psychology, there is a real need to stop the discipline becoming a natural science, and losing its social scientific moral compass. The discipline is already sold to prospective students as a natural science by many universities, and many psychologists are keen to sell themselves as scientists who do natural science: not just by wearing lab coats, but by doing controlled experiments and chasing both truth and profit. In making this case for themselves, psychologists are reportedly engaged in research that often fails the natural science test of replication (Jump, 2015). It would be better for psychologists to remember that psychology is grounded in the social in theory and in epistemology, and is a social science that needs to work across the inter-disciplinary boundaries with other social sciences such as sociology. So psychologists who want to remain social, and be critical thinkers in the radical tradition, need to build bridges back to sociology, where they will find scholars willing to support them in their battles with the positivists and would be natural scientists.

For economists seeking to turn their subject into a morally bound social science, there is much more work to be done. The neo-liberals have control of the curriculum, many universities and many learned societies around the world. To be a dissenting economist is to fight a long and often lonely struggle (Heise, 2014). Getting work published in journals and having research proposals accepted by finding bodies is very difficult for an economist who dares to question the neo-liberal consensus. For early career economists and students, they need to question the theories and models they have been taught and widen their reading to include dissenting voices and opinions (Chang, 2011). There are dissenting economists who are lucky to have tenure or well-established jobs around the world. These individuals need to do everything they possibly can to nurture the dissenting economists who are in the early stages of their careers. If necessary, other critical social scientists need to work collaboratively with the dissenters to give them moral and practical support inside universities.

From here, making the moral case looks impossible. Higher education has changed so much in the past twenty years that any manifesto

DOI: 10.1057/9781137577917.0006

for political action and resistance to neo-liberalism seems doomed to fail. I do not doubt that this book will be published and read by my colleagues, especially those who are sympathetic to my arguments, those already practically engaged in what I call critical sociology. But what about the rest of the social sciences, the rest of higher education and the wider public sphere? I don't believe there will be a deliberate capitalist conspiracy to hide this book, because hegemony is not a conspiracy. But I do think the book will be met with disdain by many readers (assuming it ever gets noticed enough to be read at all), especially this conclusion with its call for action. Do I really think people are going to change the way the world is, just because one relatively unknown British author says so? Well, I can only try to persuade people, to add my voice to those others making the same arguments (e.g., see Docherty, 2015).

But I believe there is a moment of opportunity. There is a growing number of discounted citizens in countries around the world, angry at capitalism and the power of the elites. There is a realization that equality and liberty together are being threatened as never before by these structures of power. And there are people in positions of power who may well be amenable to our cause.

At a keynote presentation at a music conference in Rotterdam in November 2014, John Street made the observation that many of the people he knew in senior leadership roles at his university were punks, or former punks. The generation that revelled against the British Establishment and embraced radical politics has now found itself holding the levers of power. My own Dean fits this trajectory, and there are countless other examples that can be found; people who took to the radical and anarchist politics of punk have now become decision makers and leaders as they reach the 'deep end' of their careers. Many of these old punks will have changed their politics, no doubt, but many will still carry a seed of that radical activism inside them. It is these people we need to target to convince them the social sciences need to be defended and promoted as the way to making the world a more equal and a fairer place.

DOI: 10.1057/9781137577917.0006

References

Adorno, T. (1991) *The Culture Industry* (London: Routledge).

Alexander, J. C. (2014) *The Antinomies of Classical Thought: Marx and Durkheim* (London: Routledge).

Arendt, H. (1973) *The Origins of Totalitarianism* (New York: Houghton Mifflin Harcourt).

Aristotle (1962) *The Politics*, translated by T. A. Sinclair (Harmondsworth: Penguin).

Bartlett, R. C. and Collins, S. D. (2011) *Aristotle's Nicomachean Ethics* (Chicago: University of Chicago Press).

Bastow, S., Dunleavy, P. and Tinkler, J. (2014) *The Impact of the Social Sciences: How Academics and Their Research Make a Difference* (London: Sage).

Bednarek, M. (2012) 'Constructing "Nerdiness": Characterisation in the Big Bang Theory', *Multilingua*, 31, 199–229.

Blackledge, P. (2006) *Reflections on the Marxist Theory of History* (Manchester: Manchester University Press).

Borch-Jacobsen, M. and Shamdasani, S. (2012) *The Freud Files: An Inquiry into the History of Psychoanalysis* (Cambridge: Cambridge University Press).

Braund, D. (1994) 'The Luxuries of Athenian Democracy', *Greece and Rome*, 41, 41–48.

Breiner, J. M., Harkness, S. S., Johnson, C. C. and Koehler, C. M. (2012) 'What Is STEM? A Discussion about Conceptions of STEM in Education and Partnerships', *School Science and Mathematics*, 112, 3–11.

DOI: 10.1057/9781137577917.0007

Brink, D. O. (1992) 'Mill's Deliberative Utilitarianism', *Philosophy and Public Affairs*, 21, 67–103.

Brown, A. (2008) 'Our Club, Our Rules: Fan Communities at FC United of Manchester', *Soccer and Society*, 9, 346–358.

Bruff, I. (2014) 'The Rise of Authoritarian Neoliberalism', *Rethinking Marxism*, 26, 113–129.

Burrow, J. W. (1985) *Gibbon* (Oxford: Oxford University Press).

Butler, J. (2006) *Gender Trouble: Feminism and the Subversion of Identity* (London: Routledge).

Bynum, W. (2013) *A Little History of Science* (New Haven: Yale University Press).

Campaign for Social Science (2015) *The Business of People: The Significance of Social Science over the Next Decade* (London: Campaign for Social Science and Sage).

Capaldi, N. (2004) *John Stuart Mill: A Biography* (Cambridge: Cambridge University Press).

Chang, H-J. (2011) *23 Things They Don't Tell You about Capitalism* (London: Penguin).

Claeys, G. (2000) 'The Survival of the Fittest and the Origins of Social Darwinism', *Journal of the History of Ideas*, 61, 223–240.

Comte, A. (1868) *The Positive Philosophy* (New York: W. Gowans).

Conservative Party (2015) *The Conservative Party Manifesto 2015* (London: Conservative Party).

Darwin, C. (1872) *The Expression of the Emotions in Man and Animals* (London: John Marry).

Darwin, C. (2009) *The Origin of Species* (London: Penguin).

Dawkins, R. (1986) *The Blind Watchmaker: Why the Evidence of Evolution Reveals a Universe without Design* (New York: W. W. Norton).

Dawkins, R. (2006) *The God Delusion* (New York: Houghton Mifflin).

Dawson, M. (2013) *Late Modernity, Individualization and Socialism: An Associational Critique of Neoliberalism* (Basingstoke: Palgrave Macmillan).

Dennett, D. (2006) *Breaking the Spell: Religion as a Natural Phenomenon* (London: Allen Lane).

Depew, D. J. and Weber, B. H. (1995) *Darwinism Evolving: Systems Dynamics and the Genealogy of Natural Selection* (Cambridge, MA: MIT Press).

Depew, D. J. and Weber, B. H. (2011) 'The Fate of Darwinism: Evolution after the Modern Synthesis', *Biological Theory*, 6, 89–102.

DOI: 10.1057/9781137577917.0007

Desmond, A., (1989) *The Politics of Evolution* (Chicago: University of Chicago Press).

Dickinson, H. W. (2010) *James Watt: Craftsman and Engineer* (Cambridge: Cambridge University Press).

Dilthey, W. (1989) *Selected Works, Volume One: Introduction to the Human Sciences* (Princeton: Princeton University Press).

Docherty, T. (2015) *Universities at War* (London: Sage).

Duncan, D. (2013) *The Life and Letters of Herbert Spencer* (Cambridge: Cambridge University Press).

Durkheim, E. (1982) *The Rule of Sociological Method* (New York: Free Press).

Ekelund Jr, R. B. and Olsen, E. S. (1973) 'Comte, Mill, and Cairnes: The Positivist-Empiricist Interlude in Late Classical Economics', *Journal of Economic Issues*, 7, 383–416.

Evans, J. A. S. (1991) *Herodotus, Explorer of the Past* (Princeton: Princeton University Press).

Fehling, D. (1988) *Herodotus and His 'Sources': Citation, Invention, and Narrative Art* (Liverpool: Francis Cairns).

Feyerabend, P. (1975) *Against Method* (London: Verso).

Flyvbjerg, B. (2001) *Making Social Science Matter: Why Social Inquiry Fails and How It Can Succeed Again* (Cambridge: Cambridge University Press).

Ford, R. and Goodwin, M. (2014) *Revolt on the Right* (London: Routledge).

Foucault, M. (1972) *The Archaeology of Knowledge* (London: Tavistock).

Foucault, M. (1973) *The Birth of the Clinic* (London: Tavistock).

Foucault, M. (1980) *Power/Knowledge, Selected Interviews and Other Writings* (New York: Pantheon).

Foucault, M. (1991) *Discipline and Punish: The Birth of the Prison* (Harmondsworth: Penguin).

Foucault, M. (2006) *The History of Madness* (London: Routledge).

Fox, R. L. (2005) *The Classical World* (Harmondsworth: Penguin).

Freese, J. (2007) 'Replication Standards for Quantitative Social Science: Why Not Sociology?', *Sociological Methods and Research*, 36, 153–172.

Freud, S. (1997) *The Interpretation of Dreams* (London: Wordsworth).

Freud, S. (2003) *Beyond the Pleasure Principle* (London: Penguin).

Freud, S. (2005) *The Unconscious* (London: Penguin).

Friedman, M. (2009) *Capitalism and Freedom* (Chicago: University of Chicago Press).

Fuller, S. (2000a) *The Governance of Science* (Milton Keynes: Open University Press).

DOI: 10.1057/9781137577917.0007

Fuller, S. (2000b) *Thomas Kuhn: A Philosophical History for Our Times* (Chicago: University of Chicago Press).

Galison, P. and Hevly, B. W. (1992) *Big Science: The Growth of Large-Scale Research* (Stanford: Stanford University Press).

Gamble, C. (2007) *Origins and Revolutions: Human Identity in Earliest Prehistory* (Cambridge: Cambridge University Press).

Gane, N. (2014) 'Sociology and Neoliberalism: A Missing History', *Sociology*, 48, 1092–1106.

Gibbon, E. (2005) *The History of the Decline and Fall of the Roman Empire*, 6 vols (reprinted in 3 vols) (London: Penguin).

Goldacre, B. (2008) *Bad Science* (London: Fourth Estate).

Goldacre, B. (2014) *Bad Pharma: How Drug Companies Mislead Doctors and Harm Patients* (New York: Macmillan).

Goonatilake, S. (1998) *Toward a Global Science: Mining Civilizational Knowledge* (Bloomington: Indiana University Press).

Gough, A. (2014) 'STEM Policy and Science Education: Scientistic Curriculum and Sociopolitical Silences', *Cultural Studies of Science Education*, 10, 445–458.

Gramsci, A. (1971) *Selections from Prison Notebooks* (London: Lawrence and Wishart).

Grant, E. (1996) *The Foundations of Modern Science in the Middle Ages: Their Religious, Institutional and Intellectual Contexts* (Cambridge: Cambridge University Press).

Guba, E. and Lincoln, Y. (1989) *Fourth Generation Evaluation* (Newbury Park: Sage).

Gutas, D. (2012) *Greek Thought, Arabic Culture: The Graeco-Arabic Translation Movement in Baghdad and Early Abbasaid Society* (London: Routledge).

Habermas, J. (1984) *The Theory of Communicative Action, Volume One: Reason and the Rationalization of Society* (Cambridge: Polity).

Habermas, J. (1987) *The Theory of Communicative Action, Volume Two: The Critique of Functionalist Reason* (Cambridge: Polity).

Habermas, J. (1989) *The Structural Transformation of the Public Sphere* (Cambridge: Polity).

Habermas, J. (1998) *The Inclusion of the Other* (Cambridge: Polity).

Habermas, J. (2000) *Post-national Constellation* (Cambridge: Polity).

Habermas, J. (2008) *Between Naturalism and Religion* (Cambridge: Polity).

Hall, A. R. (2014) *The Revolution in Science: 1500–1750* (London: Routledge).

DOI: 10.1057/9781137577917.0007

Hall, A. R. and Dunstan, G. (1954) *The Scientific Revolution, 1500–1800: The Formation of the Modern Scientific Attitude* (London: Longmans, Green).

Hall, S. (1993) 'Culture, Community, Nation', *Cultural Studies*, 7, 349–63.

Hall, S. (1995) 'Negotiating Caribbean Identities', *New Left Review*, 209, 3–14.

Hall, S. (1996) *Modernity: An Introduction to Modern Societies* (London: Blackwell).

Hall, S. (1997) 'Subjects in History: Making Diasporic Identities', in W. Lubiani (ed.) *The House that Race Built* (New York: Pantheon).

Hall, S. (2002) 'Race, Articulation, and Societies Structured in Dominance', in P. Essed and D. Goldberg (eds) *Race Critical Theories* (London: Blackwell).

Hall, S. (2011) 'The Neo-liberal Revolution', *Cultural Studies*, 25, 705–728.

Hall, S. and Jefferson, T. (1976) *Resistance through Rituals* (London: Hutchinson).

Halsey, A. H. (2004). *A History of Sociology in Britain: Science, Literature, and Society: Science, Literature, and Society* (Oxford: Oxford University Press).

Hannam, J. (2010) *God's Philosophers: How the Medieval World Laid the Foundations of Modern Science* (London: Icon).

Harari, Y. N. (2015) *Sapiens: A Brief History of Humankind* (London: Vintage).

Haraway, D. (1987) 'A Manifesto for Cyborgs: Science, Technology, and Socialist Feminism in the 1980s', *Australian Feminist Studies*, 2, 1–42.

Haraway, D. (1989) 'Situated Knowledges: The Science Question in Feminism and the Privilege of Partial Perspective', *Feminist Studies*, 14, 575–599.

Harris, S. (2004) *The End of Faith: Religion, Terror, and the Future of Reason* (New York: W.W. Norton).

Hawkins, M. (1997) *Social Darwinism in European and American Thought, 1860–1945: Nature as Model and Nature as Threat* (Cambridge: Cambridge University Press).

Heilbron, J. (2015) *French Sociology* (Ithaca: Cornell University Press).

Heise, A. (2014) 'The Future of Economics in a Lakatos–Bourdieu Framework', *International Journal of Political Economy*, 43, 70–93.

Helleiner, E. (1996) *States and the Re-emergence of Global Finance: From Bretton Woods to the 1990s* (Ithaca: Cornell University Press).

DOI: 10.1057/9781137577917.0007

Herodotus (1920) *The Histories*, translated by A. D. Godley (Cambridge, MA: Harvard University Press).

Hitchens, C. (2007) *God Is Not Great: How Religion Poisons Everything* (New York: Atlantic).

Hobbes, T. (1996) *Leviathan* (Cambridge: Cambridge University Press).

Hobsbawm, E. (1988) *The Age of Capital* (London: Abacus).

Hobsbawm, E. (1989) *The Age of Empire* (London: Abacus).

Hobsbawm, E. (1992) *Nations and Nationalism since 1780* (Cambridge: Cambridge University Press).

Inglis, D. (2014) 'Cosmopolitans and Cosmopolitanism: Between and Beyond Sociology and Political Philosophy', *Journal of Sociology*, 50, 99–114.

James, W. (1890) *The Principles of Psychology* (New York: Dover).

Jones, D. S. (2014) *Masters of the Universe: Hayek, Friedman, and the Birth of Neoliberal Politics* (Princeton: Princeton University Press).

Jump, P. (2015) 'Majority of Psychology Papers Are Not Reproducible', *Times Higher Educational Supplement*, 2219, 13.

Kahneman, D. (2011) *Thinking, Fast and Slow* (New York: Macmillan).

Kent, R. A. (1981) *A History of British Empirical Sociology* (London: Gower).

Keynes, J. M. (1936) *The General Theory of Interest, Employment and Money* (London: Macmillan).

Kitching, G. (1988) *Karl Marx and the Philosophy of Praxis* (London: Routledge).

Klein, N. (2007) *The Shock Doctrine: The Rise of Disaster Capitalism* (New York: Macmillan).

Kuhn, T. (1957) *The Copernican Revolution* (Chicago: University of Chicago Press).

Kuhn, T. (1962) *The Structure of Scientific Revolutions* (Chicago: University of Chicago Press).

Lane, M. (2015) *Plato's Progeny: How Plato and Socrates still Captivate the Modern Mind* (London: Bloomsbury Publishing).

Latour, B. (1987) *Science in Action* (Cambridge, MA: Harvard University Press).

Leaman, O. (2013) *Averroes and His Philosophy* (London: Routledge).

Lefebvre, H. (1982) *The Sociology of Marx* (New York: Columbia University Press).

Lincoln, Y. and Guba, E. (1985) *Naturalistic Inquiry* (London: Sage).

Lindberg, C. (2009) *The European Reformations* (Oxford: Blackwell).

DOI: 10.1057/9781137577917.0007

Lightman, R. (1997) *Victorian Science in Context* (Chicago: University of Chicago Press).

Lukes, S. (1982) 'Introduction', in E. Durkheim (ed.) *The Rule of Sociological Method* (New York: Free Press).

Lynd, R. S. (2015) *Knowledge for What: The Place of Social Science in American Culture* (Princeton: Princeton University Press).

Mandelbrote, S. (1993) 'A Duty of the Greatest Moment: Isaac Newton and the Writing of Biblical Criticism', *The British Journal for the History of Science*, 26, 281–302.

Marx, K. (1992) *Capital* (Harmondsworth: Penguin).

McCright, A. M. and Dunlap, R. E. (2011) 'Cool Dudes: The Denial of Climate Change among Conservative White Males in the United States', *Global Environmental Change*, 21, 1163–1172.

McDonald, J. I. H. (1998) *The Crucible of Christian Morality* (London: Routledge).

Mills, C. W. (2000) *The Sociological Imagination* (Oxford: Oxford University Press).

Millward, P. (2011) *The Global Football League: Transnational Networks, Social Movements and Sport in the New Media Age* (Basingstoke: Palgrave Macmillan).

Morford, M. P. (2002) *The Roman Philosophers: From the Time of Cato the Censor to the Death of Marcus Aurelius* (New York: Psychology Press).

O'Keefe, T. (2009) *Epicureanism* (London: Acumen).

Orwell, G. (2009) *Diaries* (London: Random House).

Packard, V. (1957) *The Hidden Persuaders* (New York: David McKay).

Paine, T. (1987) *Thomas Paine Reader* (Harmondsworth: Penguin).

Parsons, T. (1964) *The Social System* (New York: Macmillan).

Plato. (1969) *Plato in Twelve Volumes, Vols. 5 & 6: The Republic*, translated by P. Shorey (Cambridge, MA: Harvard University Press).

Polanyi, M. (1958) *Personal Knowledge: Towards a Post-critical Epistemology* (Chicago: University of Chicago Press).

Popper, K. (2005) *The Logic of Scientific Discovery* (New York: Routledge).

Potter, G. (2014) *The Philosophy of Social Science: New Perspectives* (New York: Routledge).

Pritchett, W. K. (1993) *The Liar School of Herodotus* (Amsterdam: J. G. Gieben).

Renfrew, C. (2008) *Prehistory: The Making of the Human Mind* (London: Phoenix).

Rhodes, P. J. (2003) 'Nothing to Do with Democracy: Greek Drama and the Polis', *The Journal of Hellenic Studies*, 123, 104–119.

Ruse, M. (1979) *The Darwinian Revolution: Science Red in Tooth and Claw* (Chicago: University of Chicago Press).

Russell, B. (2013) *History of Western Philosophy* (New York: Routledge).

Salkever, S. G. (2014) *Finding the Mean: Theory and Practice in Aristotelian Political Philosophy* (Princeton: Princeton University Press).

Savage, M. and Burrows, R. (2007) 'The Coming Crisis of Empirical Sociology', *Sociology*, 41, 885–899.

Scott, J. C. (2006) 'The Mission of the University: Medieval to Postmodern Transformations', *The Journal of Higher Education*, 77, 1–39.

Shapin, S. (1996) *The Scientific Revolution* (Chicago: University of Chicago Press).

Simmons, A. J. (1992) *The Lockean Theory of Rights* (Princeton: Princeton University Press).

Skinner, B. F. (1953) *Science and Human Behavior* (New York: Simon and Schuster).

Smith, A. (1776) *An Inquiry into the Wealth of Nations* (London: Strahan and Cadell).

Spencer, H. (1873) *The Study of Sociology* (London: Harry S King and Co).

Spracklen, K. (2009) *The Meaning and Purpose of Leisure: Habermas and Leisure at the End of Modernity* (Basingstoke: Palgrave Macmillan).

Spracklen, K. (2011) *Constructing Leisure: Historical and Philosophical Debates* (Basingstoke: Palgrave Macmillan).

Spracklen, K. (2013) *Whiteness and Leisure* (Basingstoke: Palgrave Macmillan).

Spracklen, K. (2015) *Digital Leisure, the Internet and Popular Culture: Communities and Identities in a Digital Age* (London: Palgrave Macmillan).

Stavrakakis, Y. and Katsambekis, G. (2014) 'Left-Wing Populism in the European Periphery: The Case of SYRIZA', *Journal of Political Ideologies*, 19, 119–142.

Sunstein, C. R. and Thaler, R. H. (2008) *Nudge: Improving Decisions about Health, Wealth, and Happiness* (London: Penguin).

Turner, F. (1993) *Contesting Cultural Authority: Essays in Victorian Intellectual Life* (Cambridge: Cambridge University Press).

DOI: 10.1057/9781137577917.0007

UKIP (2015) *Believe in Britain: UKIP Manifesto 2015* (UK Independence Party: Newton Abbot).

Urry, J. (2003) *Global Complexity* (Cambridge: Polity).

Urry, J. (2007) *Mobilities* (Cambridge: Polity).

Vallgarda, S. (2012) 'Nudge: A New and Better Way to Improve Health?', *Health Policy*, 104, 200–203.

Watson, J. B. (1930) *Behaviorism* (Chicago: University of Chicago Press).

Weber, M. (1992) *Economy and Society* (Sacramento: University of California Press).

Weber, M. (2001) *The Protestant Ethic and the Spirit of Capitalism* (London: Routledge).

Weinberg, S. (2015) *To Explain the World: The Discovery of Modern Science* (London: Allen Lane).

Weindling, P. (1993) *Health, Race and German Politics between National Unification and Nazism, 1870–1945* (Cambridge: Cambridge University Press).

Westfall, R. S. (1977) *The Construction of Modern Science: Mechanisms and Mechanics* (Cambridge: Cambridge University Press).

Westfall, R. S. (1983) *Never at Rest: A Biography of Isaac Newton* (Cambridge: Cambridge University Press).

Williams, R. (1977) *Marxism in Literature* (Oxford: Oxford University Press).

Williams, R. (1981) *Culture* (London: Fontana).

Wimmer, A. and Glick Schiller, N. (2002) 'Methodological Nationalism and Beyond: Nation-State Building, Migration and the Social Sciences', *Global Networks*, 2, 301–334.

Wiseman, R. and Watt, C. (2004) 'Measuring Superstitious Belief: Why Lucky Charms Matter', *Personality and Individual Differences*, 37, 1533–1541.

Woolgar, S. (1981) 'Interests and Explanation in the Social Study of Science', *Social Studies of Science*, 11, 365–394.

Woolgar, S. (1988) *Science, the Very Idea* (London: Routledge).

Yeo, R. (1993) *Defining Science: William Whewell, Natural Knowledge, and Public Debate in Early Victorian Britain* (Cambridge: Cambridge University Press).

Young, R. M. (1985) *Darwin's Metaphor: Nature's Place in Victorian Culture* (Cambridge: Cambridge University Press).

Žižek, S. (2010) *Living in the End Times* (London: Verso).

DOI: 10.1057/9781137577917.0007

Index

DOI: 10.1057/9781137577917.0008

Lightning Source UK Ltd.
Milton Keynes UK
UKOW04n0244181215

264851UK00009B/14/P